THE HAUNTED

THE HAUNTED

ONE FAMILY'S NIGHTMARE

ROBERT CURRAN

with Jack and Janet Smurl and Ed and Lorraine Warren

ST. MARTIN'S PRESS
NEW YORK

Special thanks and acknowledgment to Ed Gorman
for his work on this book.

THE HAUNTED: ONE FAMILY'S NIGHTMARE. Copyright © 1988 by Robert Curran,
Jack and Janet Smurl, Ed and Lorraine Warren. All rights reserved.
Printed in the United States of America.
No part of this book may be used or reproduced
in any manner whatsoever without written permission
except in the case of brief quotations
embodied in critical articles or reviews.
For information, address St. Martin's Press,
175 Fifth Avenue, New York, N.Y. 10010.
Design by M. Paul

ISBN 0-312-01440-6

Library of Congress Catalog Card Number: 87–28399

First Edition
10 9 8 7 6 5 4 3 2 1

AUTHOR'S NOTE

*T*he book that you are about to read was compiled from the testimony of the eight residents of 328–330 Chase Street, as well as twenty-eight other people who have experienced supernatural phenomena in connection with the Smurl family.

Some of the people whose names appear in this book have been given pseudonyms to protect their privacy; others have allowed their names to be used.

One character, David Wilson, is a composite of three people who have worked with Ed and Lorraine Warren. The role of this fictional character, however, is unconnected to the supernatural events that have taken place on Chase Street.

Certain minor liberties have been taken with the chronology of events, and some scenes and dialogue have been re-created in a dramatic fashion. But each event described adheres strictly to the facts related by the witnesses.

I want to express my deep appreciation to all of the people who granted tape-recorded interviews to me and provided insight into the plight of the Smurl family and to the mysterious realm of the supernatural.

These people include relatives, friends, neighbors, and acquaintances of the Smurl family, and dozens of others who gave me important information. Several Roman Catholic priests were especially helpful, as were various other clergymen and rabbis.

I'm also grateful to Mike McLane, my newsroom colleague at the *Scrantonian Tribune;* photographer Bob Ventre and his assistant, Tina Sandone; Bill Hastie, assistant curator of the Wyoming Historical and Geological Society, Wilkes-Barre; and last, but by no means least, my wife Monica, for her invaluable assistance in many aspects of this book.

Robert Curran

INTRODUCTION

*T*his book will disturb many people. Because it deals factually with proof of the demonic underworld, it will give some nightmares, and others confirmation that they themselves may be experiencing their own challenges from the dark world.

The Haunted concerns a Pennsylvania couple named Janet and Jack Smurl and their four children. For nearly three years now their home has been infested by demons or, as some prefer, it has been "haunted."

There is no doubt of this. Many people, from neighbors to journalists, have seen and heard the infestation firsthand.

Why has a demon chosen to infest the lives of the Smurls, who are religious, hard-working, and sincere people?

I wish there was an easy answer to that. Further, I wish my own attempts to exorcise their demon had been successful. But, though I've said mass in their home and have three times given the rites of exorcism, the demon always returns.

Always.

I monitor the Smurls' situation through my friends Ed and

Lorraine Warren, who first introduced me not only to the Smurls but to the realm of infestation itself. It was the Warrens who, responding to the needs of another couple whose house had been infested, helped me to understand the key role priests can play in dealing with demons.

Over the past two years, I have, usually at the request of the Warrens, performed about fifty exorcisms. Not all have been successful, the Smurls being an example.

The Haunted conveys to the reader some of the unimaginable horrors to which Janet and Jack have been subjected. It also conveys how deep and abiding religious faith can hold a family together even through the most trying of ordeals—including many kinds of violence and even rape.

For now, all we can do is look at the facts gathered in this book and contemplate them through our own experiences and prayer. Each of us, at one time or another, is confronted by evidence of the dark world, for just as God's shining work is all about us in sunlight and in the loveliness of flowers and in the joy on the faces of children, so is the dark angel's work in evidence, too, in illness and in madness and in the kind of treacherous and unending torture the Smurls have experienced.

But grim as that torture has been, there is finally a hopeful message to be found in it. Those among us who do not believe in a higher power cannot read *The Haunted* with an open mind and come away still disbelieving.

Bishop Robert McKenna, O.P.
Monroe, CT
June, 1987

Bishop McKenna is among the traditionalist priests and laity of the Catholic Church holding to her ancient ritual for Mass and the Sacraments against the reforms of the Second Vatican Council. He has a church in Monroe, Connecticut.

The History of a Curious House

A mong those who study the oc-
cult, it is generally believed that there are two ways a house may
become "infested" with demons.

One is the occurrence of a violent act that not only "invites"
spirits into the home but also allows them to lie dormant and appear
at will. Psychics insist, for example, that it is easy to feel the echoes
of a murder in a given house even decades after the act took place.

The second way a home becomes infested is more peculiar,
in that it is willful. The demon is invited in through the practice
of witchcraft or other black arts. Ed and Lorraine Warren, who
figure in both the Amityville case and in the following story, refer
to an instance where a Ouija board, used as little more than a joke,
led to a house becoming infested. Think, then, what is possible
when the person inviting dark spirits is deadly serious.

The address 328-330 Chase Street, West Pittston, Pennsylvania, belongs to a duplex built in 1896. Since that time there have

been several owners and tenants, the most recent of whom are John and Mary Smurl and their son Jack, his wife Janet, and their family.

Long before the Smurls arrived, however, there were rumors about the duplex. Residents who wish to be unnamed say that for decades there have been stories, some possibly true, others obviously fanciful, about the duplex. These people even mention that occasionally the police were called in to investigate odd occurrences, though the police have no such record of any investigations.

Even without the spectre of supernatural phenomena, West Pittston has a long history of problems. Most of the town of 10,000 is located over anthracite mines that gave the area its relative prosperity for so many decades. Tragically, the mines, now filled with water, caused many West Pittston homes to cave in. The depth of the subsidences varies. Some are six inches to a foot—one house caved sixty-four inches into the ground.

The mine cave-ins were so prevalent and dangerous in the late 1930s and early 1940s that schools had to be closed. A prelate who has spent time investigating occult matters speculates that the cave-ins may have caused demons to rise up from ground used for satanic purposes. He mentions finding pig bones beneath an excavated house. The bones were pointed in the shape of a hexagram, the sign of the devil.

Meanwhile on Chase Street . . .

When you consider the history of the duplex, you are considering nothing less than virtually half this country's history—the appearance of the telephone, electricity, the motor car, air travel, radio, World War II, the Salk vaccine, the Vietnam War, space travel . . .

Through it all the duplex on Chase Street stood, witness to generations being born and pressing on into history. In one decade you saw Model T Fords outside the duplex and the next decade a Chevy with running boards; then a 1951 Mercury coupe, and then the advent of small foreign cars.

And during most of this time, the rumors persisted. For several decades there had been tales told—whispered really—about the duplex.

One story had it that strange and terrible noises could be heard in the house even when it stood unrented and unoccupied.

Another related how parents would be foolish to let their children play near the house because certain indescribable things had been glimpsed through the parted curtains.

Then there was the hint that somewhere in the vicinity witchcraft was being practiced and that its dark powers might affect the entire neighborhood.

Rumors.

"It was the perfect place for Halloween night," a one-time resident who asks to remain anonymous says. "Think of yourself as a little kid. There's a full moon and jack-o'-lanterns in all the windows and then there's this one house with this really strange kind of grip on the whole neighborhood. At dinner sometimes you heard your parents talking about it but they didn't know any more than you did, really. Just that it was alleged that satanic things went on there sometimes. So on Halloween night—" he laughs and even today there's a certain edge of anxiety in his voice. "Well, I've never been sure if there was something wrong with the house or not. All I knew was that when I got close to it, I had this eerie sensation that this wasn't like any other house."

Rumors.

Nothing you could prove or disprove.

But still they persisted.

And in 1985 the rumors would at last be proved true.

Coming of Age

*T*he coal region of Pennsylvania was long on grief and short on justice.

Approximately 500 square miles of the state bore one of the richest treasures of all, anthracite, the best of all coals because it offers the highest percentage of fixed carbon and the lowest volatile content. It also gives the greatest heating power, burns slowly, and sends neither soot nor smoke into the air.

Fortunes were made on the brilliant black coal so rich in the area around Wilkes-Barre, Scranton, Hazelton, and Pottsville but many of them were fortunes made on the backs of poor immigrants, the Irish (the largest group), Poles, Ukrainians, Czechs, and Italians. For every spanking new railroad car housing a flamboyant millionaire, for every sparkling white mansion, there were hundreds of men and children down in the depths of the earth, risking and often losing their lives for a pittance.

As a result, the coal mining area quickly became violent with strikes and civil disorders. Martial law was declared many times as miners, tired of toiling for pennies and seeing sons and fathers die in the hazardous bowels of the earth, decided it was better to bloody themselves against state troopers than continue on in miserable poverty.

Only gradually did wages improve.

Only gradually were safety guidelines established.

Only gradually did it become illegal for children (some of them as young as five) to work in the mines.

Only gradually.

It was said that the nineteenth-century American immigrant brought two things with him to the New World—empty pockets and an almost belligerent allegiance to the Roman Catholic Church, as the Protestant overlords of the time discovered to their dismay.

Each ethnic group had its own church—one for Poles, one for Czechs, one for the Irish. In addition to a belief in the supremacy of the Vatican, these groups held one other matter in common: an unspoken but deeply held fear of the supernatural. In the old country such things were talked about openly and with wary respect; here, during the time of the Industrial Revolution, with cold hard science the master of all, such beliefs marked you as low in both position and education. In the era of mass production, surgery, and the steam locomotive, only a fool would speculate on the existence of ghosts and werewolves and vampires.

And yet within the confines of their churches, with the red and blue and green votive candles casting long shadows, old women with coarse scarves on their heads whispered of just such things, and passed down their beliefs to children and grandchildren.

If you grew up in Pennsylvania's coal-mining region, you quickly learned that the statesman-philosopher Emerson had not been exaggerating when he said that self-reliance was the most important virtue of all.

For one thing, well into the present century, the immigrant families tended to have large broods of children, which meant that the children had to learn early on to work and work hard, not only to help their parents but to insure their own survival. Necessity forced many immigrant children to leave school by the fourth or fifth grade to take full-time jobs like delivering groceries to the "right" side of town for five cents an hour until their "opportunity" to work in the mine came along, as it inevitably did.

But life in the area was not as grim as certain journalists of that time chose to portray it. For one thing, the ethnic groups had brought across the ocean a great sense of ritual and fun. On nights of the harvest moon you heard accordion music and the clatter of dancing feet. On Christmas Eve, at midnight mass, you heard the beautiful voices of a children's choir singing in Latin about the baby Jesus. And on summer days, along the river banks, you saw shy young lovers strolling through the green grass of the new season. You were taught respect for your elders, you were taught the value of hard work, you were taught that America bestowed blessings that no other country ever could, and you were taught that you should gladly die to defend your country or your family. These were the rules you learned to live by and you took them with you down into the mines and you took them with you to the boisterous taverns on Friday nights, and you took them with you to your deathbed, where, your children and grandchildren gathered round you, you passed on to succeeding generations the same truths you had lived with all your life.

After World War II, there were some changes.

The young men who had gone to Europe and the Pacific to fight for their country did not return quite the same people.

At first, the elders in the immigrant communities considered their changed attitude to be little more than a reaction to all the bloodshed and travail they had witnessed.

But after a few years, you could see that the men who had fought in the war had in fact subtly separated themselves from the ways of their parents.

To be sure, they had not lost their belief in hard work, in honesty, in religious faith, or in unquestioning loyalty to the government. But they gradually began to express dreams that their parents, bound by tradition and by bitter memories of labor wars and the depression, could only consider foolhardy.

Many of the men back from the war said that they did not want to work in the mines. Many of them said that they wanted the type of colorful, prefabricated house they saw being built in Levittown and elsewhere. Many of them said that they planned for each and every one of their children to go to college and never have to settle for the hardscrabble lives preceding generations had been forced to live.

Times were changing and so was the thinking of an entire generation of working-class people. If the land barons and the oil barons and the political brokers wanted their privileges, they would damn well have to start paying for them.

The year Jack Smurl graduated from high school, the following songs were in the top ten: "Smoke Gets in Your Eyes," "Mack the Knife," and the inevitable hit by Elvis Presley, "A Big Hunk o' Love."

The year Jack graduated from high school, Dwight David Eisenhower was still president, the Yankees expected to win the pennant, and America was racing to catch up with Russia's space effort.

This was in Luzerne County where Jack's father worked as a welder for a steel company and where his mother tried to help Jack decide what he wanted to do about his future, now that graduation time was at hand.

Jack, who'd been blessed with a high IQ, could easily go on to college or he could pursue any number of occupations where, in those days, college was not mandatory. A relaxed boy, good at sports, who liked to roam the countryside especially when autumn graced the hills with its beautiful colors, Jack had enjoyed his school years at a Catholic school in Wilkes-Barre, but he did not relish the prospect of more studying. His easy-going exterior concealed an adventurous heart. After school he'd occasionally check out the offices where the various branches of the military kept recruiters. He came home one day with the news that he was going to enlist in the navy. His parents felt what most parents do at such moments: happiness that their child is pleased with himself, uneasiness about the world at large and how cruel and indifferent it can be to young people.

Jack Smurl took into the navy the ethic of his upbringing in the coal-mining country: He worked hard, he obeyed orders, he made the right kind of friends (avoiding troublemakers and chronic complainers), and he chose for himself a service occupation that demanded not only skill but sensitivity. He was a neuropsychiatric technician assisting doctors with electroshock treatment.

Even today, electroshock therapy is a controversial procedure. Electroconvulsive therapy (ECT) simply means passing an electric current into a human brain for a very brief time; this will presumably lift the patient's depression or reduce suicidal tendencies. Though ECT has proved successful, there are still many psychotherapists who consider it barbaric and only nominally useful in treating the long-term effects of mental illness.

Jack saw how many men were helped by the treatments, which was one reason he took such pride in his job. He also saw, for the first time, how reality and unreality could be confused by a mind uncertain of its own stability. He would remember this when his own life, several years later, took an ominous turn.

Jack's navy career taught him that the world is comprised of a variety of peoples and that one must learn tolerance for their different ways. It also showed him a fundamental truth he'd secretly suspected all along: that he liked the mining country of Pennsylvania and that despite dreams of wanderlust, he wished to return there when his navy days were over.

Which was what he did.

He arrived back in Luzerne County and took up the life of a young man with aspirations for a good job, a loving wife and family, and some of the perks he'd observed while traveling around during his navy years. He knew there was only one thing that could reap all these benefits—hard work.

And so he started in.

During Jack's tenure in the navy, a girl named Janet Dmohoski was attending public high school in Duryea, near West Pittston.

Janet, a pretty girl given a somewhat intellectual look by her large oval eyeglasses, liked all the things most of her peers did, though she had no interest in the drugs or promiscuity favored by the "hippie" movement, the sweeping social revolution that was then forming.

Raised by her mother after a difficult divorce, Janet, like most teenagers in the area, was expected to help out with housework (her mother was a senior citizen affairs director for a retirement home) and to keep up with her homework whatever else might be going on—boys calling, or dances being held, or "dreamy" movies at the local picture show (this was the era of the innocent beach party pictures, Frankie and Annette).

In addition to music, Janet enjoyed nature walks and talking long hours with friends about all the hottest high school news, and thinking about various possible futures for herself. During her junior and senior years, she considered many different careers. But even then she knew that raising children would be the best of duties, not only a sacred responsibility (as her Catholic faith taught her) but a privilege as well. Janet loved to hold infants, play with them, watch their wet little mouths open gleefully as you tickled or teased them.

The year Janet graduated from Northeast High School the top three records were "Downtown," "You've Lost That Lovin' Feeling," and "This Diamond Ring." To show how "the times were a'changin' " a record called "The Eve of Destruction," an anti-Vietnam war anthem, was right behind the other, frothier tunes.

The night of Janet's graduation, she celebrated along with the other students, feeling happy and pleasantly more mature and eager to see what life held for her. Shortly thereafter, Janet went to work in the packaging department of a local confectionery company.

Even though Jack worked there, the two didn't meet until 1967 at a Christmas party.

A Life Together

*F*or the nation, Christmastime 1967 was an especially bitter time. Several Johnson administration officials had begun to see that the war in Southeast Asia would not be won, and the violence on college campuses continued to grow worse. President Johnson, delivering a Yuletide speech, was said to look, in the words of one reporter, "like a man haunted by his own sins."

For Jack Smurl, however, life was better than it had ever been. His job at the confectionery company promised promotions and higher salary. His health was good, his body strong and lean, not unlike that of the movie star some said he resembled, Charles Bronson. He had many friends and enjoyed sports of all kinds as well as an occasional night drinking 3.2 beers with his fellow workers.

There was only one thing that nagged at Jack, who was then twenty-seven, and that was the fact that he was still unmarried. In this part of the country, men generally got married and started families in their early twenties. Though there had been a few women who had struck Jack as marriage possibilities, he had still not met the one with whom a lifetime bond seemed worthwhile.

Christmas that year was a time of buying presents for his parents and his sister, of attending parties and getting ready for the onslaught of relatives with whom he always shared the holidays.

It was also time for the traditional company party, and it was there that he met the woman he would marry one year later, Janet Dmohoski.

"I think I knew right away," Janet recounts today. "I really liked the way he presented himself and the respect he had not just for me but for all the things I valued. He had a great sense of humor but he never let it become cruel or obscene the way some men sometimes get."

"The funny thing was," Jack points out, "that we'd worked for the same company for some time but had never met. Friends of ours kept saying 'Be sure to go to the company party tonight,' and it sure was a good thing I did because otherwise I might never have met Janet."

Janet: "We shared a lot of the same beliefs. We were both Catholics. We believed in the work ethic. We didn't go along with so many people our age who were into drugs and protest. We both wanted a family and we both wanted to make sure that the family would be raised properly."

That winter was their first season of courtship—a time when ice glazed the trees like silver fire in the afternoon sun, when snowmen with pot bellies and carrots for noses greeted them from the softly rolling hills, and when cheeks and fingers got numb from the cold.

Janet: "It was just right, our courtship. It moved along very quickly but not too quickly. We took the time to get to know each other and to get to know our likes and dislikes. I think that's why our marriage has been so strong. We used our courtship to iron out the few real differences we had." She laughs. "And we had a great time doing it."

Movies, dances, parties were elements of the courtship but so were meetings with groups that helped out the community. Jack would later become a celebrated member of the local Lions club, just as Janet would become equally busy as a Lioness.

Buds appeared on the trees; grass became green. In the coal-mining region of Pennsylvania the spring hills are an unfurling mixture of foliage and rock, with soils among the richest in the eastern part of the country, ranging from limestone to shale. Picnic and camping areas abound, and Jack and Janet discovered another mutual interest, the outdoors. While Pennsylvania yielded nearly $3 billion in anthracite and other minerals annually in the 1970s, it also produced a net annual saw timber cut of 575 million board feet. Rivers, lakes, and rolling land give the countryside beauty, and trees such as spruce, white pine, birch, hickory, and black walnut give it uniqueness. The forests and campgrounds and river edges that Janet and Jack roamed were abundant with animal life, too. The couple enjoyed the portentous spectacle of black bears and the grace of white-tailed deer. For those who liked to fish there were streams filled with catfish and bass and trout—all you could ask for.

Then it was autumn and the hills blazed with the ironic loveliness of a countryside about to die. There were harvest dances celebrating legends and myths brought over long ago from the old country, and there were the increasingly intense plans for the wedding, now that it had been officially announced and approved by both families.

While both Janet and Jack still felt the wonderful rush of new love, they also felt their affection deepening into solid trust and kinship. Parents and fellow employees alike were happy for the couple and expressed this by giving them exuberant showers, dinners, and parties.

Janet and Jack, being Catholic, received marital instructions from one of the local parish priests, and then awaited the day both of them had dreamed about for nearly a year now.

November, and the first snow; the sky drab with the darkest of autumn months. But not even November could ruin the glow burning constant within them.

Finally, Christmastime, its real significance the birth of the Christ child in the shabby surroundings of a stable more than 2,000 years ago—a significance not lost on December 28, 1968, the day of their marriage.

Jack: "Being Catholic, I believe that marriage is a sacrament, in the literal sense a sacred experience. And that's how we've always treated it."

There was something touching about seeing people who labored all day with their hands dressed up in colorful gowns and tuxedos, red or white boutonnieres on the lapels of the men, corsages of gardenias or roses on the women. And everywhere you looked you saw the continuity of which the coal-mining region was so proud—the children, the next generation—dancing jigs to the music along with their grandparents and generally having the run of the hall. At the windows the winter light waned and night fell and the music lost its raucous edge and became more frankly sentimental. Then husbands found the arms of their wives and renewed their love by dancing to songs such as "Harbor Lights," "Tennessee Waltz," and "The Christmas Song."

And when you looked around that night you saw a very special couple, the center of attention for at least this day. Jack and Janet Smurl were now man and wife.

Moving into Trouble

*T*he first years of their marriage were especially pleasant ones for Jack and Janet Smurl. Their first two girls, Dawn and Heather, came along, Janet gave up her job and became a full-time housewife, and Jack found himself progressing in terms both of pay and prestige at the company where he worked. They lived with Jack's parents, John and Mary Smurl, in a house in Wilkes-Barre.

Then, in 1972, Hurricane Agnes invaded northeastern Pennsylvania and the house where the two families lived was flooded with twelve feet of water. Though John and Mary renovated the Wilkes-Barre house, the local redevelopment authority took it over and forced them to move.

It was then that John and Mary bought a duplex at 328-330 Chase Street in West Pittston, a nearby town of 10,000, for $18,000 in the fall of 1973. Chase Street is narrow and runs perpendicular to Wyoming Avenue, a few blocks from the town's only shopping center, Insalaco's. There are several older duplexes on the northern side of the street, with newer single-family homes dominating the other side. It is a model working-class neighborhood: clean, well kept, American flags vivid in the daylight of national holidays.

At the time they purchased the home, John and Mary Smurl knew little about the previous occupants except that the 328 side was owned by an elderly man and had been vacant for several years and that 330 was owned by an elderly woman who had rented it to tenants. They made all the appropriate checks on the house— plumbing, lighting, foundation, termites, liens—and found everything in order. In the fall of 1973, they moved in.

During this same period, the elder Smurls sold the northern side of the duplex to Jack and Janet for a price far below market value, $4,000. Delighted and happier than they'd ever been, Jack and Janet and their two daughters moved into 328 Chase Street on October 1, 1973.

Life in West Pittston was even better than their previous married years had been. Janet became active in the community and helped form the West Pittston Lionesses club, serving as its first president. She was also one of the organizers of the local chapter of Students Against Drunk Driving at the Wyoming Area High School.

Jack and Janet participated together in community activities as well. The couple helped form a girls' softball league and they worked long hours on the Cherry Blossom Festival, which aided community civic and youth groups. Jack was active in the West Pittston Lions club and was club secretary for two years.

For the first eighteen months at their new address their hours were filled with kids and grocery shopping and mass and civic group meetings and long, long hours of work: Janet at ironing board and sink and stove, Jack at the plant where he was on his way to a mid-management position.

Those who knew the Smurls in that first eighteen-month period said they'd rarely known happier couples. You had to look back to the dreams of the previous generations in anthracite country to understand what Jack and Janet had come to symbolize—success. Not flashy cars, not a dissolute and selfish life-style, not trendy clothes and trendy thinking, but success as this part of the country understood it—they toiled long, they paid their bills, their family was the center of their lives, their belief in God grew stronger yearly, and they were willing to extend through their civic activities the kind of charity that Christ taught was necessary for a holy life. You could see all this, their neighbors would tell you, in the way Jack, when he arrived home, would sweep up and hug and kiss his wife and his kids.

Eighteen months of the kind of happiness many long for but few achieve.

Such happiness that they didn't really think much about certain peculiar things that began happening inside 328 and 330 Chase Street.

THE STAIN

In January of 1974 Mary Smurl purchased a new red carpet. When the workers from the rug company laid it out in the living room, Mary discovered that the rug contained a large, round grease stain.

That night, John and Mary used a cleaning solution on the rug and the stain came out completely. But two days later when they came downstairs for breakfast, they discovered that the stain had reappeared. There began a frustrating and somewhat unnerving process: John and Mary would clean off the stain only to have it appear again a few days later. Ultimately they took the rug to the town dump, bought a new carpet, and had no problems with it.

THE TV SET

Jack Smurl is a western movie fan. He is a particular admirer of John Wayne, whose portrait hangs in his living room. Tired from a long day's work, Jack was at the TV set one night in 1974 enjoying a western film when suddenly the set, without giving any advance warning, burst into flame, the way it might had a plastique bomb been thrown at it. Part of it melted in flame and smoke before Jack could get the fire out.

The TV fire was followed by many other inexplicable blazes around the Smurl household. A new electric stove caught fire shortly after it was purchased. The wiring in Jack Smurl's brand new car similarly crackled into flame only days after he bought it.

LEAKING JOINTS

During the massive renovation both families did on the duplex during 1974, John Smurl, an experienced welder, soldered thirty joints in copper tubing for the water pipes. When Jack turned the water on, however, all the joints leaked. Mystified, John Smurl soldered the pipes a second time. They leaked again.

This mysterious occurrence was followed by other minor but irritating problems. Repair jobs that should normally have taken ten minutes suddenly became major projects that took hours. Plumbing problems were constant. One drainpipe that both John and Jack worked on had to be repaired five times before it finally became usable.

STRANGE MARKINGS

Jack and Janet took special pride in how they'd remodeled their bathroom. Among other things, they installed a new sink and bathtub. But they awakened the morning after they finished their remodeling work to find that the porcelain sink and tub had been scratched beyond repair, chips of it knocked out. The sight was ugly and disturbing, as if the talons of some frenzied beast had clawed at the porcelain.

The evidence of this scratching continued. Several times Jack painted woodwork and trim near the ceiling, only to find, in the morning, claw marks raked across the previous night's work.

DAWN'S TERROR

Dawn Smurl had always been athletic, intelligent, and not given to the sort of fanciful imaginings many young people enjoy. From the start she'd been a great help to her mother around the house and a diligent student at school. When she became upset over something, Jack and Janet knew that there must be a good reason.

During 1975 Dawn several times ran into her parents' bedroom screaming that she'd just seen people floating around in her room. Each time, Jack would go to Dawn's room and investigate, but he was unable to find anything.

SMALL IRRITATIONS

By 1977, the Smurls were aware that their house was "spooked" in some way. That they found many of the incidents amusing attested to their common sense and religious faith.

The toilet flushed many times, for example, when no one was in the bathroom.

Radios turned on, blaring, even though they weren't plugged in.

Jack Smurl heard footsteps upstairs, and drawers opening and closing in two of the bedrooms. He was home alone at the time.

Over the next four years, as the family grew by two members (the twins Shannon and Carin were born in 1977), the strange events continued.

In the early morning hours, Jack and Janet heard lawn chairs creaking on their front porch, as if people were rocking in them. After hearing the creaking three times, the Smurls went downstairs to investigate. They found the chairs empty but moving, as if invisible inhabitants were sitting in them.

One night Jack was lying in bed when he felt a gentle caress on his shoulders. He assumed that his wife was being romantic. Yet when he turned to her, he found her asleep.

For most of 1983 the Smurl household smelled sourly of some foul but inexplicable odor. At first the girls joked that it was Jack's "smelly feet." But no matter how the family searched, they could neither find the odor's source nor rid the house of it. What Jack recalls, thinking back, is that the odor first appeared during a time when he was kneeling before his bed, saying the rosary.

The curious house would grow even more curious as the weeks and months went by.

And Janet and Jack Smurl would begin a frustrating ten-month search for help that would only make them feel more isolated and afraid. Janet, for example, contacted the Department of

Mines to see if some of the strange things happening in the house might be the result of the process known as subsidence. The person at mines told the Smurls to check their foundation for evidence of cracks or crumbling. But none was found. Once more, they had searched in vain for an explanation of what was happening to them.

Encounter with a Dark Form

Janet smiled to herself. She wondered if it was illegal to sniff the big red plastic bottle of Era Plus, her laundry detergent of choice and one that she found pleasant to smell.

The time was winter and she was alone in the basement. Upstairs the TV set could be heard faintly; a game show audience was laughing about something, and then applauding. During drab winter months Janet found television a good companion while doing housework.

While she loaded the washer, she debated what she would make for dinner tonight. One thing about the Smurls, she thought to herself; you didn't have to worry about fancy dishes. The Smurl family liked a meal made up of the basics—meat, potatoes, vegetables. Such food not only tasted good, it was also the easiest way for Janet to make sure that her family got essential vitamins and nutrients.

She had just loaded the washer when she heard it.

Or thought she heard it.

Her name being called.

She pushed the washer door shut and stood straight up, a pretty woman of thirty-seven dressed in a work shirt and slacks.

Her pulse raced and she felt the first faint trace of sweat along her brow.

She had the distinct impression that someone had called her name.

She looked around the laundry. A green plastic laundry basket sat in the east corner, cardboard boxes containing such things as Christmas ornaments and some of the children's old clothes lay in the west corner.

"Janet."

This time her fear was icy and visceral. She knew that her name had been called, and she also knew that she was no longer alone in the basement.

She glanced up at the small square window, at the slate gray day filling it. She smelled the Era Plus again and heard the rasp of the dryer and the slight thudding of the washer. These were things of the real world and they should not allow for her name being called out of thin air by some presence, yet that's exactly what was happening.

"Janet."

This time the voice came from behind her.

She spun around. Nothing. Empty air.

"Janet."

The same voice. Soft. Female. Eerie.

How could this be happening in the middle of the afternoon with the lights on, she wondered.

"Janet."

All she could do was stare at the area from which the voice seemed to emanate.

Once again a strong sense that she was not alone caused her heartbeat to increase. She decided there was only one thing she could do. Speak back.

"What do you want?" she asked.

But the only answer she got was the usual basement noises—washer and dryer.

She had once watched a "Donahue" show on which a woman who had been raped said that afterward she had felt completely violated, and in a real way that was how Janet felt at this moment, as if her home were no longer her own, as if the dread that had gone largely unspoken among the Smurl families had now been proved conclusively to be justified.

Something terrible really was going on in the duplex.

"Janet."

"WHAT DO YOU WANT?" Janet screamed.

Did she imagine that the voice softly laughed, seeming to take pleasure in Janet's panic and confusion?

But again there was no answer.

Janet ran a trembling hand through her hair and took a deep, calming breath.

She moved away from the washer and through a shadowy section of the basement to the stairs.

Upstairs the game show audience was laughing and applauding again.

She went up the stairs backward, one step at a time, keeping her eyes on the familiar laundry area.

No hint of any ghostly shape troubled the air.

No disembodied voice floated up to call her name.

She wondered for a moment if she had imagined it. Perhaps all the small annoyances and mysteries about this house had finally gotten to her and she'd simply given in to her imagination.

"Janet."

This time when the voice came, she turned around and ran up the stairs, slamming the door behind her.

She could not wait to reach her bedroom, where she kept a special rosary her mother had given her; she fell to her knees right in the kitchen.

She bowed her head and prayed that the Lord would free this house from whatever troubles were presently being visited on it.

She prayed long into the afternoon, both on her knees and walking through the house, until early winter dusk splashed long shadows through the house, and the girls at last burst through the door with laughter bright as sunlight and diverting tales of their day at school.

Over the past few months, Jack and Janet Smurl had many times discussed the increasing number of odd events in their home. They had already openly mentioned the possibility that their house might be "haunted," but they were still not quite ready to concede that this was in fact the source of their trouble.

Whenever possible, for example, they looked for natural and logical explanations to explain away the mysterious activities. When they could, for example, they laughed at some of the quirkier occurrences, like the time when, despite the thermostat reading 70, the house had been cold as a meat locker. Or the time (not at all funny) that Jack's parents had heard foul and abusive language coming from Jack and Janet's side of the duplex, but Janet and Jack had not been arguing or using profanity. Mary Smurl later admitted it took her several months to believe otherwise.

On the night following the incident in the basement, Janet Smurl talked to her husband about how frightening it had been to hear her own name called, and to feel the chill presence of something unworldly in the basement with her.

Jack did not doubt her at all.

Janet then said what they seemed to take turns saying. "We've got to get some help."

Both the Smurls distrusted many people associated with so-called occult phenomena, seeing them as nothing more than charlatans. As religious people, the Smurls had no trouble believing in another realm of existence, and believing that realm sometimes touched this plane of existence, yet the investigating they'd done had led nowhere. Several people had recommended "experts" to the Smurls but these experts all smacked of theatricality and greed.

"I'm really going to start looking, Jack," Janet Smurl told her husband that night.

"I'll start asking around, too."

Janet said something she never had before. "I—I'm getting scared."

Jack reached across the kitchen table and took her hand. Their eyes held. His voice was scarcely a whisper. "So am I." He looked around at the new refrigerator and stove and recently remodeled kitchen, the labors of their hard work. It all felt unfamiliar and somewhat dangerous now—their own home—and because of forces they could not in the least comprehend.

Jack lit a cigarette, stirred sugar into his coffee. "It's almost every day now, isn't it?"

She nodded. "Yes. Maybe nothing big. But every day there's something."

Jack exhaled and shook his head. Janet recognized the pride and belligerence in the gesture. "Nothing's going to run us out of here, hon. You wait and see. Nothing."

On that note of determination, they went to bed.

Despite her talk with Jack, Janet's fear and anxiety did not lift. Even the children began to notice it.

"Mom, are you all right?" Dawn asked at breakfast two days later.

"I'm fine, honey."

Dawn followed her mother into the kitchen and sat down at the Formica table in the center of the small room, obviously sensing that Janet was avoiding the subject of her mood.

"Basketball practice tonight?" Janet stood at the sink and talked to her daughter over her shoulder.

"Yes," Dawn said but without her usual enthusiasm. "Right after school as usual." Dawn abruptly changed the subject. "Mom, you're not answering my question."

"What question is that, honey?"

"You know. About your mood the past few days."

26

She turned around and faced her daughter. She smiled as earnestly as possible. "Honey, I'm fine. Really." She forced a laugh. "The older you get, the stranger you get."

But Dawn wouldn't be mollified. "I'm worried about you, mom. I really am."

Janet shrugged. "Honey, I'm fine. Really."

She smiled at Dawn and thought how proud she was of her. Dawn was becoming quite an attractive young lady, one who balanced energy with intelligence and real sensitivity to the needs of others. Dawn enjoyed school, had a boyfriend the family liked, and was an outstanding player on the girls' basketball team. You couldn't ask much more of a daughter than that.

"Are your sisters ready for school?" Janet asked.

"Heather is," Dawn said, referring to her twelve-year-old sister. "But Shannon and Carin are arguing in the bathroom."

"How about hurrying them along?"

Dawn gave her mother one more lingering melancholy glance and then stood up. "All right," she said softly and left the room.

"Shannon! Carin!" Dawn cried as she went up the stairs leading to the bedrooms where the seven-year-old twins managed to dawdle each morning while getting ready for school.

At the sink, Janet finished with the dishes that Dawn had used to fix lunch for herself and the twins to take to school. She raised her gaze to the grim gray sky outside. It was 7:30 A.M. but it might as well have been twilight. If only the world was as cheerful a place as the disk jockey on the radio claimed it was. She thought again of the voice that had called to her. Had it been imaginary?

When she'd come upstairs from the basement, fleeing the sound, she had forced herself to walk through the house and check every room, in every closet, under every bed, to make sure no one was there hiding from her.

She'd found no one.

Nothing.

Could she have imagined the voice? It was so real. But what other explanation was there?

Janet shuddered and resolved to think of other things as the girls burst from their bedrooms upstairs and pounded down the steps, ready at last for school.

As was their custom, Janet bent for each child to kiss her goodbye—Dawn first, then Heather, and then the twins.

At the front door, Dawn took her mother's hand and said, "Why don't you go buy yourself a nice blouse or something today, mom? Maybe it'd do you good to get out of the house."

Janet smiled, squeezed Dawn's hand in return. "You know, maybe you've got something there, hon. Maybe getting out of the house would be a good thing for me."

Dawn gave her a thumbs up. "Go for it, mom."

Then the girls were off to school.

The nearby mall was crowded with shoppers. Snowy days always seemed to bring out hundreds of people.

Janet looked through several shops, enjoying her leisurely morning, had a Bismarck and a cup of coffee at a small doughnut shop, and then went back home without buying herself anything. The trip out of the house had buoyed her spirits just as much as a blouse would.

At home, Janet pulled the ironing board out of the kitchen closet and turned on the radio to a soft rock station. Then she set to work, pulling clothes from the large plastic basket brimming with the daily wear of all sizes, shapes and colors needed by a family of six—everything from socks (argyles were back in style for the girls) to underwear (nothing fancy; just the kind you bought at Penney and Sears) to shirts (housewives, Janet noted humorously, should say a prayer every once in a while for the inventor of permanent press; even if you did have to touch up the "permanent" part with an iron now and then, it was still a lot easier than the old days).

While she was working and letting her mind drift she felt a sudden chill in the room, as if a window had abruptly been opened to the cold February air.

The chill forced her to look up, and it was then that she saw the thing.

"I stayed very calm," Janet later recounted. "In the movies people always scream and run, but I just stood with the iron still in my hand and watched the thing. To be honest, I wasn't sure at first whether it even existed. I knew there was a possibility that I was hallucinating or something. But then it started moving toward me, and I knew then that there was no doubt about it—the thing, whatever it was, was real. Very real."

The creature was a black human-shaped form. A cape fluttered from its back. But what was most upsetting was that the face had no features at all.

The more closely Janet looked, the more she saw that the creature was not one of true substance. It appeared to be made of a thick dark rolling smoke, not solid at all. She could see right through it. An odd but not offensive odor lay on the air. The creature stood approximately five-feet-nine-inches tall (Janet measured it against the height of the refrigerator) and seemed to glide rather than walk.

It passed close by her, the chill and the odor more overpowering now. It rushed through the kitchen and into the living room.

At first she was paralyzed. "I didn't realize it then, but I'm sure I was suffering from clinical shock," Janet later recounted. "All I could do was stand there and sort of blink my eyes at where the creature had been. I can remember how hard my heart was beating and how I couldn't even work a good scream up in my throat. I was just—paralyzed is the only word."

After a full minute had passed, Janet glanced down at her hand and saw the hot iron that she was still holding. She carefully propped it up on the ironing board and took slow, careful steps toward the living room.

She stood quietly in the doorway between the kitchen and living room.

No one was there. The house was silent.

Janet walked into the living room and looked around. Nothing. Just like the other day after she'd heard the female voice calling her name.

She glanced around the room. For the first time since the Smurls had moved in here, Janet began to see all the possible hiding places that burglars—or creatures of any description— might use.

The house that had been her pride now gave another hint that it could also hide possibly ominous secrets.

Standing rigidly in the middle of the living room, her arms folded protectively in front of her, Janet drew in a shaky breath and blinked back the tears.

Janet often visited her in-laws on the other side of the duplex. There were two reasons for this. First, John and Mary Smurl had become dear and intimate friends. Second, Mary Smurl had for many months been ailing from a variety of illnesses (mere months later she would suffer a heart attack).

Twenty minutes after the frightening black shape had passed through her house, Janet went to visit her mother-in-law. She was determined to discuss frankly the experience she'd just had. With most other people, Janet would have been apprehensive about revealing such things. But she knew that Mary would listen calmly and reasonably and might even have some suggestions about what Janet should do.

"As it turned out, she was the one who surprised me," Janet Smurl says today. "I ran over to Mary's side—I must have looked half-crazy as I came through her door, my eyes wild from what I'd just witnessed. I remember I kept trying to think of how I was going to bring up the subject. 'Mary, I think I just saw a demon from hell'? You know, I didn't want to sound crazy. I didn't want her to think that I was losing my mind or anything. And that's when she completely surprised me."

Janet Smurl had scarcely gotten inside Mary's duplex when she noticed that the older woman was acting odd. Usually Mary had a quick smile for her, and the offer of coffee and a roll. But today the older woman sat stiffly in a wooden, Colonial-style rocking chair with a multicolored afghan draped over its back, and scarcely acknowledged Janet's presence.

Janet sat down and lit a Salem, burning herself on the match. She was still so rattled from what she'd seen that she could not quite focus herself.

Janet: "You know how you get after something very bad has happened—you just can't quite bring yourself back to reality. I'd come over here to tell Mary what had happened but then I realized I didn't know how I was going to say it. Bring it up, I mean."

But Janet needn't have worried.

Mary Smurl, leaning forward in the rocking chair, looking pale, said, "I have to tell you something, Janet."

"That's funny. That's why I came over here. To tell *you* something."

"I still can't quite believe it."

Janet noticed how taut Mary's hands had become as they gripped the arms of the rocking chair. Janet sensed terrible fear and confusion in her mother-in-law and then she wondered if the black form might not have come over here, too.

Mary said, "Maybe you won't even believe me, Janet. I don't know if *I* believe me. Maybe I'm getting old. Maybe I'm getting—" she shook her head. "There was this thing—this black thing—I don't know what else to call it. It came through the wall and—"

Janet: "I laughed. I couldn't help myself. I was releasing this incredible tension. Here I'd been afraid of telling Mary what had happened to me and it turned out that she'd just had the very same experience."

Mary made the sign of the cross, held up one of the novena cards she used to pray with every afternoon. "I was sitting here in my chair, with my feet up, saying my novenas when I felt some kind of presence. I looked up and saw this black form appear, walking from the stairway and down into the living room. It walked past me and disappeared. I thought my eyes were playing tricks on me." She shook her head, almost more mournful than frightened. "What could it have been?"

Janet shrugged. "I don't know." Then she thought about the inevitable conversation she'd have with her husband Jack tonight. "Jack's going to ask us a lot of questions when we tell him."

Mary nodded. Her son was very inquisitive and liked to know all the details. He'd been that way as a boy and remained that way as a man. Which was why Janet thought it would be a good idea for them to tell each other exactly what they had seen.

Janet: "I felt that by talking through what we'd both just experienced, maybe we could have a better idea of what was going on. By the time we finished talking, my arms were covered with goosebumps. And I'll tell you why. It wasn't because of the black shape. It was because I suddenly realized how very familiar things—Mary's couch and TV set and rocking chair, for example—can suddenly become very threatening objects. We never really *look* at what's around us until something terrible happens and then things assume very different shape and meaning. I sat there and watched the snow fall outside the window and looked over at the TV screen where I was used to seeing a baseball game or Dan Rather on the news—and suddenly it all seemed very threatening somehow, as if I couldn't trust my instincts about anything anymore. You believe the world is one thing and then you sense all of a sudden that it's very different and that there is a lot going on we don't see or at least don't understand. I didn't want to upset Mary by talking about it anymore, so I thanked her for sharing her experience with me and then I went back to my side of the house to wait for Jack, who usually got home around five."

When they got home from school, the older girls, Dawn and Heather, found their mother in a curious mood—withdrawn, somehow, and nervous. And overly protective in a way that they couldn't understand, hugging them for no apparent reason, and even getting tears in her eyes when she did so.

"Mom, are you all right?" Dawn asked.

"I'm fine," Janet Smurl said. But she said it too quickly, and Dawn and Heather knew it.

At one point Heather peeked into her parents' bedroom and found her mother on her knees, a rosary entwined in her fingers.

Five o'clock could not come soon enough.

Deadly Evidence

*F*or several weeks after that, very little untoward happened in the Smurl household.

To be sure, there remained those minor "accidents" that could logically be attributed to natural explanations—lights blinking on and off; the occasional door or closet slamming in an empty room—but Janet and Jack began to relax, and thus so did their children.

The four girls had certainly become aware of the strain the curious events of the past few months had put on their parents. Jack, the gentlest of men, began losing his temper. Janet, normally easy-going, showed anxiety when the smallest part of her household routine went wrong. (Between themselves, they'd even wondered once if the girls might not be playing tricks on them, which could explain some of the odd events. But almost immediately they rejected the idea, knowing that while the girls were occasionally mischievous, they would not do things that would upset or worry their parents this way.) The Smurls were still the strong, loving parents they'd always been, but obviously they were preoccupied with the "visitor" and the other related incidents.

But as gray February became sunny March, boding well for an early spring, Jack and Janet returned to their former selves. Jack got his promotion at the plant, Janet received an award for all her service work with the Lionesses, and the girls got involved in various athletic endeavors, everything from basketball to volleyball to swimming.

One night during this peaceful time, Janet and Jack were sitting up watching the late news on television when Janet said, "Do you suppose it's over?"

She did not have to define for Jack what "it" was.

"I'm almost afraid to say it, but I think it is," Jack said, and smiled. "I think the spooks got themselves a room at the Holiday Inn."

Earnestly, she said, "You really believe it's over?"

"I really do."

"And you're not just saying that?"

"I'm not just saying that."

That spring Heather Smurl was thirteen years old, the age at which most Roman Catholic children are confirmed. The confirmation process is one through which the participant becomes aware, in an adult way, of the tenets and responsibilities of being a good Catholic. In some respects it is like the bar mitzvah of the Jewish religion.

The ceremony was scheduled for a week night evening, which meant there was a great deal of rushing around in the house. Janet Smurl had made dinner, pressed Heather's white confirmation dress, talked to Shannon about a test she'd only gotten a C on, and finally corralled Heather long enough to pin a special collar on her special dress.

This was in the kitchen.

"You know how things are when you're rushed," Janet Smurl

recounts. "Heather and I were in the middle of the kitchen and Shannon was standing off to the right, over by the refrigerator, and that's when it happened."

As she worked on her daughter's dress, a massive tearing sound, as if something had ripped through a wall, filled the kitchen. Before there was time to move, Janet glanced up to see the heavy ceiling light they'd installed seven years ago when they remodeled their home come crashing down amidst sputtering electrical blinking and powdery ceiling dust.

Janet and the girls screamed and tried to get out of the light's way. Janet and Heather were fortunate. They managed to get under the kitchen table.

But before Heather could pull her sister to safety, Shannon was struck on the shoulder by the four-foot-long ceiling light as it crashed to the floor.

By now Jack, who had been getting ready upstairs, had come racing into the kitchen, terrified by what he'd heard. Heather and Shannon were sobbing. Janet was examining Shannon to determine the extent of her injury.

"My God," Jack Smurl said, looking up at where the light had been. He knew that it had been properly fitted there and securely bolted.

But now there was just a ragged hole showing white plaster and the entrails of black electrical wiring that curved thickly like snakes, and hung exposed.

Janet's mind was fixed on the moment that light had fallen within two inches of Shannon's head. If the girl had been struck by it directly, she would have been killed.

Shannon could have been dead. . . .

Quickly, the Smurls got their daughters ready to pile into the van and drive to Immaculate Conception Church for confirmation. They were already running seriously behind time.

On the way out the door, the children going on ahead of them, Janet Smurl glanced at Jack.

No words were necessary to convey what she was feeling.

The terror.

Jack pulled her to him and kissed her gently on the cheek. "It'll be all right, babe."

Huddled into him, she closed her eyes and allowed herself the luxury of a shiver. "I'm really scared."

By this time Janet knew enough about the supernatural to know that sanctified events and objects made demons particularly angry. What could be more sanctified than confirmation?

Janet's eyes rose to the ugly hole where the light fixture had been. Aloud, she prayed to the Lord Jesus that whatever might happen to her and Jack, the children would not be hurt.

Then Janet felt the stirrings of a new feeling as well—the beginning of cold hatred for the presence that was filling their house. It had now tried to hurt one of her children.

Janet: "After that, we spent hours, days, weeks, talking to people who might possibly be able to help us. But I have to say that most of the people we mentioned this to took a very condescending attitude. For instance, I called several universities all over the country that had departments dealing with either parapsychology or paranormal phenomena. But surprisingly they weren't much help at all. I remember one especially bad experience where the professor, in a haughty tone, asked me if I watched a lot of horror movies, implying that I'd just let my imagination run away with me. I just couldn't believe it."

Jack's Nightmare

*N*ear the end of April, Jack and Janet Smurl packed their camper with kids and various supplies and set off to one of the campgrounds where, on weekends, they relaxed and enjoyed their leisure time.

The springlike weather had continued through April, apple blossoms scenting the air, grass stretching like a green ocean up the rolling foothills of the region.

After the ceiling light had injured Shannon, Jack and Janet began to see the true dimensions of their problem. While as yet they did not believe in hauntings as such, they had come to understand that some unnatural force was working within the walls of their home. What it was, or what motivated it, remained a mystery.

All the Smurls knew was that on this sunny weekend they wanted to escape its clutches, so they headed for the camping ground.

* * *

Chase Street is in the best sense a real neighborhood. The people who live there watch out for each other. When a family goes out of town, the other neighbors keep at least a casual eye on the empty house, making sure that nothing happens to it.

The weekend the Smurls left, several neighbors checked on the house, saw that everything appeared to be all right, and then went on to their own homes.

Just after dark on Saturday night, however, several neighbors heard something that still frightens them. A neighbor who requests that his name not be used says, "I've never heard anybody scream as they were dying, but I imagine that the sound I heard coming from the Smurls' home must sound very much like that. The way people must have sounded in concentration camps or something. I was walking past the Smurls' home when I heard this very strange fluttering sound coming from the second story window—like giant birds flapping their wings or something. Then the screaming started and it was real scary. My wife went on home ahead of me. She was too frightened to stay once the screaming began. Like I say, you would have thought somebody was being axed to death or something inside that house. But we knew that it was empty, that the Smurls were out of town."

This was the first time the neighborhood at large became aware of the problems the Smurls were having with their house.

Unfortunately, several other neighbors would later understand all too well.

Three of the girls needed school clothes. They were at the age when they seemed to outgrow their entire wardrobe in the space of six months.

Tonight, on this warm May evening, Janet decided to take all four of the girls to the Insalaco shopping center, near the southern edge of town.

Jack, tired from the day's work and feeling that he might be coming down with the flu, said he would just stay home and probably go to bed early.

He took a paperback biography of John Wayne upstairs with him and laid down. The time was 7:14. Reading proved to be the perfect sleeping potion because after only three pages, the paperback fell to his chest and Jack promptly went to sleep.

As a boy, Jack had often had dreams of falling from tall buildings. He could still recall the sensation of being suspended in air and then crashing toward the pavement below. He always awoke with a start, his heart pounding hard in his chest.

Tonight he had the sensation of being suspended in air but not of falling. It was as if he were literally lying on the air currents, comfortable and tranquil.

Only gradually did Jack begin to realize that he was not, in fact, dreaming.

There was the sound of cars going by in the street outside.

There was the aroma of spring flowers through the open window.

There was the feel of his clothing against his flesh.

Suddenly, he opened his eyes and saw that he was not dreaming at all. He was levitating, lying perfectly still two feet above his bed.

His first reaction was panic. He started to move, to thrash around, trying to sit up right there in the middle of the air. It was then that the thing hurled him back onto the bed.

He jumped from the bed and stood with his hands clenched into fists, shouting, "Show yourself! Show yourself!"

But there was just his own hammering heart. And the peculiar, mocking silence.

He had become a plaything for the entity loose in this house, and at this moment he was more afraid than he ever had been in his life.

Interview with Jack Smurl

Q. Did you have any inkling at this point that things were only going to get worse?

A. Not really. [Pause] Look, I'm a family man in my forties. I've had a very normal background. When I was a boy my dad used to take us swimming and I played basketball and I hung out at the Catholic Youth Center, especially on the nights when they had dances there—[laughs] you know, lots of Elvis and Johnny Mathis and Nat "King" Cole records. Then I did my hitch in the navy (in those days you called a short hitch like mine a "kiddie cruise") and then I got out and got married and had a family.

Q. So you're saying that you didn't have anything in your background to prepare you for this?

A. Exactly.

Q. So you didn't have any idea of what to make of it?

A. No, and I'd argue that most people wouldn't. The first thing the average person does is *reject* the idea that he's dealing with the supernatural. All these things happen to you—really incredible things—but your mind keeps looking for some *normal* explanation. You know?

Q. So at this point you rejected the possibility that you were dealing with the supernatural?

A. No, I didn't reject it. I just hoped some other explanation would come along. But of course when I sat down and really thought about it—black forms that walked through walls and light fixtures that fell down and nearly killed my daughter—what other explanation could there be?

Q. So deep down you knew you were dealing with the supernatural but you kept trying to deny it?

A. Yeah. That's a good way to put it. It was this whole denial process. Only, as things kept happening, it was harder and harder to keeping saying it's not supernatural. Because no other explanation was possible. Not a one.

Statement of Lenora Brinser, Age Twenty-three

*I'*ve lived down the street from the Smurls for seven years and my parents are two of Janet and Jack's best friends.

Most of our neighborhood became aware of what was going on at the Smurl house after the weekend when the screaming was heard by several nearby residents. After that, Janet and Jack were much more forthright in discussing the problems they were having with those of us who lived nearby.

At first, I admit I was very skeptical. Though I consider myself a religious person, I see many occult and supernatural occurrences as either "tricks" of some kind by publicity-seekers or the mind playing tricks on itself.

But because so many things were happening to the Smurls, I saw the possibility that paranormal things could happen, even right on my own block.

As for the Smurls themselves, all of us could see the strain this was putting on them. Sometimes Janet and Jack would bicker a bit and we'd never seen that before; and occasionally Jack would sort of snap at his daughters, who were really his pride and joy, so snapping at them was very uncharacteristic.

Janet began to confide in my mother a great deal and since I was still living at home, I was part of many conversations.

Somehow, though I believed that Janet believed everything she was saying, I still had reservations of my own.

I guess I was still looking for some kind of natural explanation, even though, along with most of the other neighbors on West Chase Street, I was starting to see that any kind of natural explanation was highly unlikely.

One afternoon, after work, I came home and found Janet and my mother talking about how Janet's mother-in-law Mary had heard children laughing and running around in the Smurls' half of the duplex, even though none of the Smurls were there at the time.

I guess that struck me as pretty humorous, for some reason, because I said, "Don't worry Janet, I'll call the ghostbusters and have them ghostbust the house for you.

I could see instantly that I'd embarrassed my mother and hurt Janet's feelings.

I quickly apologized and said, "I guess it isn't funny any more, is it?"

Janet's humor returned. "Maybe we should do what they used to in the movies—you know, offer you a big prize to stay in our house one night. Then I think you'd change your mind."

"I really don't think I'd be afraid," I said confidently.

Gently, Janet said, "I think you'd change your mind, Lenora."

We had coffee and some home-baked chocolate chip cookies to go with it and talked some more about all the strange things that had been happening at the Smurls' and then it was time for Janet to go start making the family dinner, and for my mother to go to her ceramics class, after which she'd meet my father at a restaurant.

I planned to stay around the house and wash the dishes. I

stood at the top of the steps as my father and mother left. My father closed the front door and locked it. I then turned on the stereo and began to do the dishes. Not five minutes went by when the music—rock and roll—was so loud it hurt my ears. I went over to the radio and turned it back down, assuming there was a short in the radio wires.

When I turned around the front door was open about two or three inches. I walked down to it and saw the lock was still engaged.

The presence or being that Janet had been talking about these past months was now in our house, too. I could feel it and sense it in the air, which had a peculiar texture, different somehow from what it usually was.

And all I could think was that Janet had brought "it" with her.

Then I did something that I shouldn't have done. I went to the phone, in tears and panic, and called Janet. I could hear my own voice—and even though I wanted to stop myself from saying such cruel words, I couldn't.

"You brought it with you! It is in *our* house now!" I cried. "I don't want you to ever come here again, Janet." My whole body shook and I was sobbing from fear and confusion.

Fortunately, Janet and I remained friends because she understood what I was going through, the awful things that terror can make you say to people.

Just after the being had filled my own living room, there was another lull at the Smurls. You could see Janet and Jack becoming more relaxed again, and you could see this in the girls, too, because they'd been under a lot of strain also.

When the neighbors talked now, it was with optimism. Maybe what had happened to the Smurls was coming to an end.

Maybe the worst was behind us, and I say "us" because nearly the entire block was involved by this time, either in witnessing strange events or in trying to comfort and help the Smurls in their ordeal.

But we were wrong.

This was not the end, it was only the beginning.

45

The Violent Night

*O*n a June evening of 1985, just after she had finished making love with her husband, Janet Smurl was pulled by some invisible fury from her bed and dragged across the floor.

Janet: "Mostly I just remember the sound of my own screaming. One moment I'd been lying in Jack's arms and the next something I couldn't see had grabbed my right leg."

Jack: "It was like a tug of war going on. I was holding onto her as hard as I could because I had no idea what the thing wanted to do to her. But the harder I tried to keep her next to me, the harder it pulled on her."

Suddenly, Jack was paralyzed. "Literally," he says, "I couldn't move. Something had seized control of me. I couldn't even curse the thing. I was totally immobilized."

Janet: "I held onto both Jack and the bedclothes—it was like clinging for my life on the edge of a cliff. I'd never felt more vulnerable, exposed the way I was, in my life. I just kept screaming for help. But somehow I managed to stay on the bed."

Terrified to consider what might happen to her next, Janet was startled to find that the invisible force abruptly gave up.

Janet: "I felt the pressure leave my leg. And then I saw Jack starting to move again. He put his hand out to me and I touched it. And that's when the banging started."

For more than a year, the Smurls had heard banging and pounding inside their walls, as if an army of demons was enraged. But it had never been as loud as it was tonight.

Then the odor came, foul as a city dump on a steaming hot day but twice as oppressive.

Janet: "I began to gag, literally. And I could hardly breathe. I'd never been overpowered by an odor this way before."

Jack: "The sounds and the odor really began to make me feel as if I was losing my mind. I was dizzy and sick and I had this pounding headache. Somehow I managed to get hold of Janet's hand and we got out of there. It was like trying to escape from a burning building, only in this case the flames and the smoke were invisible."

The pounding in the walls continued, as if the entity that had taken control of the house wanted to prove its dominance and mock them.

During the next few days, Janet was uncharacteristically moody and quiet. A feeling of dread filled her and no matter what she did, she could not rid herself of it, even when she thought back to her relatively carefree youth.

As a girl, Janet had been given to solitary walks through the countryside, she liked to roller skate and swim, and she spent many joyful hours in her room reading novels by the dozen, among them the Nancy Drew and Bobbsey Twins series.

Later, in high school, her taste in books changed to bestsellers and incidents based on real history. It was at this time that she'd really bloomed, becoming both a majorette and a member of the glee club.

She had fond memories of times following high school, her courtship with Jack, and their early married years. Even Carin being born with deformed vertebrae (and virtually going in and out of the hospital every month at first) had not sapped her strength the way the odd events on Chase Street did.

Janet: "I started thinking about my past—you know how everything seems so much better in retrospect, so much easier— and I guess that's what scared me and made me so depressed. I felt that my family was being threatened by something we couldn't comprehend, let alone fight. It was very discouraging."

Since girlhood, Janet had been a big fan of sit-coms—everything from Abbot and Costello and "Gilligan's Island" in the old days to "Mary Tyler Moore" and "Bob Newhart" in more recent times—and so she tried over the next few days to spend as much time in front of the TV as possible, hoping to work herself into a better frame of mind.

But none of her old standbys helped.

There was just the gray leaden skies and this terrible feeling that they were trapped in something they could never escape from.

Continuing her tireless quest for help, Janet did two things during this period. She contacted the light company to see if they could explain why the lights were going on and off, and she wrote a letter to Channel 16, detailing what was going on in the Smurl household.

The man who came from the light company and checked everything said that the house had been rewired only a few years ago and that there were plenty of circuits and that there would be no reason for lights going on and off.

And as for the television station, not a word of response. Janet fell into one of her moods of isolation again.

The Assault

*P*sychologists know that stress can destroy family life. The increase in the national divorce rate attests to how right they are: These days 50 percent of American marriages end in divorce.

Imagine then the stress Janet and Jack Smurl and their family experienced as the invisible forces that had taken over their home conspired now to destroy it.

Following the terrifying night in which Janet had been pulled from her bed by unseen hands, there ensued several weeks that tested the very foundation of the Smurl family.

Janet: "There would be periods when we were obviously in some kind of true struggle with the powers that were trying to take over our home. We got in the habit of calling it 'It.' We didn't know any other name that would be appropriate. Anyway, one day I got so tired of being frightened that I got angry. I started screaming for it to leave my house and quit intimidating my family. I suppose I must have looked very strange, standing there shouting at something I couldn't even see.

"This was the day after Jack had his St. Jude medal taken from around his neck while he slept. It had to be lifted off because it doesn't have a clasp. We felt this was just the spirit trying to show us its superiority again—proving that it was our master. The next day would be one of the worst yet because that was when it went after Simon."

FAMILY FRIEND

Simon is a big friendly dog who has been with the Smurl family since he was a puppy. He proves that not all German shepherds are violent. Each of the Smurl children has a favorite Simon story, some cute tale about the happy, protective dog as it grew to become a full-fledged member of the family.

It was the dog's gentle nature that made what happened one Tuesday morning so infuriating.

Janet was in the kitchen doing dishes, Simon sprawled out by her feet, when suddenly she saw Simon lifted from the floor by invisible hands and smashed against the kitchen door. The dog howled in pain as it crashed to the floor.

Janet dove for Simon, hugging him, trying to protect him from any more assaults. The big animal trembled and whimpered in her grasp.

But that was not the only thing It had in mind for Simon.

Soon after, Janet was in the kitchen alone again with Simon when she saw him abruptly buckle and begin to yelp in pain. His body then went into convulsive twitches, as if he were being flayed. The animal's fitful cries filled Janet's ears with pain, because she was unable to help the dog. Once more, all she could do was crouch next to Simon and hold him, and thereby keep the evil at bay.

THE PHANTOM PUPPY

The dog that a few days later figured in the lives of Mary and John Smurl, on the other side of the duplex, was anything but a family friend.

At night the elderly couple liked to have a few snacks and watch television. On this particular evening, however, Mary was alone in the living room. John was in the kitchen, repairing an appliance.

Mary, engrossed in a show, noticed the strange sight only peripherally at first. Then her head snapped around and she felt her mouth drop open.

A puppy with neither a head nor a tail ran across the room right in front of her and dashed under the love seat.

Mary hurried to tell her husband, who immediately called for Jack to help him search for the phantom puppy. The pursuit went nowhere. The puppy was not to be found. Jack measured the space between love seat and floor—one-half inch. "No puppy could go under there, mom."

"No real puppy," Mary Smurl said, feeling a shiver travel the length of her spine. Then she thought of a remark she'd made earlier that evening. To her husband she said, "Remember how I said that the incidents had been tapering off?"

John Smurl nodded.

"I'll bet this is its way of proving that I was wrong," Mary Smurl said.

Her husband and son believed she was right.

The forces in the house seemed to take real delight in tormenting them.

THE CHILDREN

Janet and Jack knew that for all the stress the haunting had put on them, the children were the ones who really suffered.

You're a nice, normal girl. You like school, sports, music, and life with your family. You're proud of your parents and the kind of people they are, and you're proud of the part they play in the community.

But over a period of less than two years your life goes from the sunny days of an average childhood to the dark and brooding days of some very disturbing events.

Do most children ever have to face the spectacle of pots and pans that fly around in the air of their own volition?

Do most children ever have to face watching their pillow being punched violently by some invisible hand?

Do most children ever have to face hearing eerie scratching, like something clawing inside the walls?

The answer, obviously, is no.

Yet the Smurl children were subjected to terrifying supernatural phenomena daily.

Janet: "One day I really lost my temper. Carin had been bothered in her room by this fluttering sound—the sound of huge birds taking flight—and it scared her so much, she ran downstairs and into my arms. After I comforted her, I ran up the stairs and went into the twins' room and really threatened. 'You leave my children alone, dammit!' I shouted. There were no more fluttering sounds that day."

The children talked among themselves, of course, about the events plaguing their house.

Dawn: "Some of it you could get used to. But some of it you just couldn't. The sound of fluttering wings, for example, is incredible. You get this image of gigantic birds taking off. One day we heard it in the chimney. My dad asked Heather to go outside and look on the roof. She didn't see anything but we could still hear the fluttering, like something was trying to claw its way into the attic. It was horrible."

Heather: "One thing we learned about was the value of prayer. Lots of times it was real hard not to give in to despair—or not just sort of run out of the house crying—but we always found that prayer could calm us down and keep us from being confused and upset the way the spirits wanted us to be. We knew it wanted to break us up and we just weren't going to let it."

But no matter how strong the Smurls' determination, there were moments when no amount of faith seemed sufficient to hold up under the demonic onslaught.

SHANNON'S FALL

Like her twin sister Carin, Shannon Smurl had always demonstrated creative abilities beyond her age. When she put Crayolas to coloring book, for instance, her work was impeccable. She also showed a knack for poetry and a talent for singing.

Shannon, age eight, slept in the top bunk above her sister. One Thursday night during the early siege, she had been tucked into bed as usual by both parents and then fell quickly to sleep.

A few hours later Jack and Janet went to bed. They had been asleep for less than half an hour when they were awakened by a loud thudding noise, as if something very heavy had been dropped from the top of the stairs to the landing below.

Startled, they then heard Shannon cry out in the darkness.

Janet and Jack raced frantically down the steps, where they found their daughter slammed into the corner.

"Honey," Janet asked, after they had determined that Shannon was all right physically. "Did you trip on the stairs?"

Jack thought this would be impossible. Both he and his wife were light sleepers. They would have heard Shannon's footsteps creaking on the old floors.

"I don't know, I don't know," Shannon said, weeping softly.

They put her back in bed, said prayers by her bedside, and then checked on the other children, who were all right.

Back in their own bed, Janet said, "I won't stand for it anymore, Jack. We've got to find some help."

Jack agreed. He had been leery of "occultists" because of their tendency to be charlatans, but now he knew that something had to be done.

His mind filled with an image of his daughter Shannon thrown down the stairs, crumpled at the bottom like a broken doll.

He had no doubt of who had done this. Or why. Once more, it wanted to prove its dominance.

But Jack and Janet Smurl had very different thoughts in mind. In the morning, the search for guidance began in earnest.

The Search for Help

*T*he neighborhood in general was well aware of what was going on in the Smurl duplex.

Most neighbors were helpful. "Even though they didn't really understand what was going on—and neither did we, of course—they were very supportive of our whole family," Janet said.

Jack: "This is one way you find out who your true friends really are. Certainly we had neighbors who were skeptical, particularly at first, and we even had a few who hinted they might like to see us move, but in general the neighbors talked with us about it and tried to come to some sort of peace with it."

However understanding people were, though, the fact remained that the Smurls' duplex remained under siege.

Occurrences as various as the hissing of invisible snakes scaring the children, and heavy footsteps thudding across the attic, and a bedspread being shredded as if by a clawed beast, continued to make the duplex a danger zone for habitation.

THE LIBRARY

In the course of the siege, Janet Smurl decided she needed to become as much of an expert on the supernatural as possible.

Daily, whatever the weather, whatever else she had to do, she went to the local library.

"They didn't have as many books on the subject as I'd have liked," Janet laughed. "But then who would have? When you really begin investigating the subject you realize that while there's really a lot of literature on demonology, there still wasn't any sort of adequate explanation for what was happening to my family."

As for the books themselves, Janet noted, "Some of them were very serious. Others were really just sensational tales and weren't all that helpful. But one thing was for sure. I learned very quickly that we weren't the only people who'd ever been plagued by demons. There were several books that documented infestations similar to ours."

The entire family took comfort from Janet's reading. "Knowing that others had gone through the same thing and survived it gave us encouragement. Jack even joked at one point that maybe we should form some kind of club. That's one thing the press distorted later on. Through most of the days and nights, however bad they sometimes got, our family kept its faith and humor. Many of the incidents we'd laugh about." Then Janet pauses. "Of course some of them were too frightening to laugh about."

At this point Janet shakes her head soberly. "During the heaviest part of my library visits a very strange mist filled half of our room one night. I woke up and saw it and tried to rouse Jack but I couldn't. We learned later that he was in a deep 'psychic sleep,' one I guess the thing had put him in. The mist stretched like a kind of webbing from our bed all the way out the window. In the moonlight, it had a very ghostly appearance. A few nights later the same thing happened again and this time I did manage to get

Jack awake. We watched as the mist swirled into a very strange shape and suddenly we realized that it had drawn itself into the shape of a person. Then it moved quickly into the closet and was gone."

Janet found no reference to such a mist in any of the books she read. She did not sleep well for several nights.

*T*WO *P*RIESTS

During the worst part of that siege, two priests were invited to the Smurl duplex.

Father Raymond L. Karsiak, a long-time family friend, came to have dinner one evening and the Smurls told him about the problems they'd been experiencing.

They were relieved to find that their friend took their words seriously.

Janet: "Father Karsiak went upstairs and then he told us that he realized he was in the presence of something evil. He said, 'You're nice, normal people and this shouldn't be happening to you.'"

As the priest talked, Janet could see that he had begun to sweat and was becoming very nervous. "We had the sense that the presence was applying pressure on Father Karsiak to leave our house."

Nonetheless, the priest went through the house, blessing each room and commanding the demon to "leave these people alone!"

At one point the pressure became so much on the priest, and he looked so shaken, that Janet and Jack were afraid he might pass out. But Father Karsiak bravely finished the blessing, then had some coffee in the kitchen with the couple, and left.

To their surprise and delight, the Smurls found that for the three days following the blessing, their home was untroubled by the demon.

Several weeks later, the demon trying once again to dominate the Smurls, the couple called on Monsignor Francis Kane to come bless the duplex.

This followed an especially troubling incident in which Mary Smurl, whose health remained bad, found herself lifted, along with her mattress, so high in the air that she was forced to jump from the levitated bed, badly bruising her knees. Her husband, who was out playing cards, became angry when Mary related the story and he helped Jack and Mary reach their decision to call the monsignor.

Janet: "Like Father Karsiak, the monsignor went through the house and blessed each room with holy water. Again, we were dealing with a man who believed absolutely in what we told him. We learned later that not all church officials would be so cooperative."

Once again they found that blessing the house kept the demon at bay for several days.

Unfortunately, its return was signaled when closet doors began opening and banging shut at will.

THE DIARY

Janet found a surprising number of sympathetic people with whom to discuss her problem. One such person was a university researcher who had spent most of his life investigating the paranormal. He suggested that the Smurls keep note of everything in a diary, which the family then proceeded to do.

Jack: "The diary gave us a record. It also showed us certain patterns, how things we did could cause it to appear again. We found out, for example, that if we were very upset about something, the entity would draw energy from us and use it against us. So we tried very hard to stay calm."

Janet: "It was during this period that we first talked of going public, of maybe calling a nearby TV station. But then we thought, 'If we went public, people would think that we were either crazy or making this up.' "

Fortunately, it was at this time that Janet received one of the most important phone calls of her life.

A Phone Call

Janet liked standing in the sunny kitchen. Even though strange things had happened during the daylight, still there was something reassuring about the way golden beams washed over the spotless appliances and the clean floor and were trapped in the starched white curtains.

This was January 1986, and the cold temperature outside only made Janet feel more secure inside.

She had taken a break from her housework and was sitting in the kitchen having a cup of coffee and a cigarette when the phone rang.

It was a friend of hers from just outside town, Carla Davies. "Hi, Janet, how are things going?"

"Oh, you know, the usual," Janet laughed. "Pots and pans flying around in the air and demons hiding in our basement."

Carla laughed appreciatively. Janet had confided virtually everything to her over the past year. Carla had no trouble believing

Janet's stories because Carla had always had an interest in the occult and supernatural. "I may have some good news for you."

"Ed McMahon is sending us ten million dollars."

"Even better."

"Seriously?"

"Seriously. I was reading this article last night about this professor at Marywood College in Scranton. He knows a lot about what the article calls 'demonic infestation.' He may be able to help you."

Janet thought of Jack's skepticism about such people. You had to be very careful not to be used or exploited by people seeking money or publicity or both.

"He's a professor?"

"Yes," Carla said.

"I guess I should give him a call."

"It sure couldn't hurt."

"He doesn't sound—"

Carla laughed. "He sounds perfectly sane."

"I'm going to do that, Carla. And thanks for the information."

"Good luck, Janet. I'll be saying a prayer for you."

Virtually every day Janet read about the subject of demonic infestation. Virtually every day Janet sought help for her and her family by asking questions of those supposedly knowledgeable on such subjects.

Finally, some good luck came her way when the same local professor told her about a couple named Ed and Lorraine Warren.

"They're professional psychic researchers," the professor said. "They've even been hired by the United States Army."

"Really?"

Janet felt thrilled and frightened at the same time. These people sounded perfect, but would they help the Smurls? "Do you think they'd listen to us?"

"Oh, I'm sure they'd listen to you. But they're usually very busy, very much in demand, and the other thing is that before they take on a case they go to great lengths to authenticate it."

Janet smiled. "If they spent an hour in our house, they'd know we're not trying to deceive anybody."

"I'm sure that's the case. Would you like their number?"

"Oh, very much. Very much."

He gave her the number.

The Warrens

*A*s demonologists, people who have devoted their lives to the study of demonic manifestations and infestations, Ed and Lorraine Warren are unequaled.

Both presently in their early sixties, they have been married for more than forty years. Ed is currently director of the New England Society for Psychic Research. His interest in the subject dates back to when the house he was raised in proved to be haunted. As a child, he witnessed objects flying around his house and he even saw apparitions.

Lorraine's experience with the paranormal also began at an early age. As a girl she saw lights around people's heads. Later she understood these lights to be auras. She had a similar experience when she met Ed: "The night I was introduced to him, I saw a sixteen-year-old athletic young man standing in front of me but then I flashed forward, glimpsed the future, and saw a heavier, graying man and I knew this was Ed at a future date. I also knew that I would spend my entire life with him."

Ed and Lorraine met during World War II. Ed went to art school, while Lorraine was a self-taught artist. They were married during the war on one of Ed's leaves. Their daughter, Judy, was born while Ed was still in the service. Later, they traveled around the countryside in a '33 Chevrolet Daisy with a German shepherd in the back seat. They supported themselves by selling their paintings. "We like to think of ourselves as the first hippies," Ed has said humorously.

"But our interest in hauntings and demonology remained constant. We traveled all over New England. Whenever we heard of something peculiar happening, we'd drive over there and investigate," he added.

"Over the years we gathered a reputation as very serious students of such occurrences. Through all our exposure to demons, we also began to learn how to deal with them."

In recent years, the Warrens were involved in perhaps the most celebrated case of demonic infestation: Amityville. While they express displeasure with the fact that "many things were exaggerated or left out of that book," they see the story of the Lutzes in Amityville as making believers of many former skeptics.

The Warrens work only with ordained clergy in attempting to drive demons from homes. "We work with every denomination, from priests and rabbis to ministers, and even Muslims."

Three books have been written on the work of the Warrens— *Deliver Us from Evil* by Gerald Sawyer, *The Devil in Connecticut* by Gerald Brittle, and *The Demonologist*, also by Brittle. In addition, hundreds of articles and two TV shows of their own have further brought the Warrens to public attention. A few years ago, NBC made a TV movie based on one of the Warrens' cases. Even academia has beckoned, Ed and Lorraine having taught at Southern Connecticut State University.

"We have a single message we want to get across to the people—that there is a demonic underworld and that on some occasions it can be a terrifying problem for people," Lorraine recently told a college audience.

One of their most notable assignments came when General George Knowlton of West Point asked them to come in and deal with a haunting that had badly shaken up many cadets at the Point in 1973.

The Smurls could have no better helpmates than this dedicated team of demonologists.

ED WARREN:

The day we drove from Monroe, Connecticut to the Smurls' home in West Pittston was overcast, with heavy dark clouds banked low on the horizon. We usually drive our van and we did so that day, the wind gusts catching us on Interstate 84, and pushing the van around on long stretches of the concrete. I remember Rosemary Frueh, who is a registered nurse and a psychic who is a member of our research team, leaning forward and laughing about how the van was getting tossed around. "Maybe I should have worn my crash helmet today."

We pulled up to the Smurls' home around one-thirty that afternoon and just sat there looking at it. When you've investigated more than three thousand cases of the supernatural in the United States and Europe, you get a certain sense of houses even from the exterior.

So we sat as cars passed by, as people hurried by, huddled into their winter coats against the sharp wind, and we watched the duplex for a time. On the way over we had discussed our phone conversations with the Smurls and had pretty much sensed that there were signals here of a serious haunting. At the least we felt their phone calls warranted a serious investigation.

Now I looked at both my wife and Rosemary.

"You getting anything?"

"Nothing in particular," Lorraine said. She is a trance medium with strong powers of clairvoyance and ESP.

"Rosemary?"

"Me, neither."

"All right. Let's go in, then."

The family that greeted us was not the sort we were used to seeing in hauntings. There was a classic pattern—troubled homelife, great domestic anxiety—but right away we knew that this family did not fit that pattern.

Jack Smurl was a strapping man, hearty and open; Janet Smurl was a friendly, soft-spoken person with luminous eyes and a ready smile. The children were neatly dressed, polite, attentive.

Over coffee we discussed the layout of the duplex, how each side had an attic, three bedrooms and a bathroom on the second floor, a living room and kitchen on the first floor, and a concrete cellar. There's a front porch and a back porch, and a two-car garage in the back. The property is enclosed by a chain-link fence.

As we talked about ourselves—responding to various questions they had about us and how we worked—I saw a look of approval in the faces of Lorraine and Rosemary. They liked the Smurls, finding in them none of the frustration and anger we saw in so many families we worked with.

The most obvious explanation for their relative calmness was their strong religious beliefs. Families who do not have God to rely on are often shattered by demonic experiences.

Janet brought more coffee as the shadows grew deeper in the late afternoon. Then I pointed to the tape recorder I'd set up and said, "Now when I first turn this on, you're going to feel a little self-conscious. But you'll get used to it. It's important that we interview you at length and then study the tapes later. All right?"

Janet and Jack looked at each other. Then they nodded and I switched on the recorder.

For the first part of the interview, Janet did much of the responding.

"Are you familiar with the term Satanism?"
"Yes."
"What does it mean to you?"
"Worshiping Satan?"
"Yes." Pause. "Have you ever practiced Satanism?"
Janet flushed. "No."
"You know what a Ouija board is?"
"Yes."
"Have you ever experimented with one?"
"No."
"Has any member of your family ever experimented with one?"
"No."
"You're certain?"
Janet glanced around at her family. "Yes, I'm certain."
"Do you read books on witchcraft?"
"Since our problems started here, I've read every book I could on the subject."
"But you have not practiced any of the rituals in the books?"
"No."
"And your faith in God has remained intact?"
"If anything, it's stronger than ever."
"The same for you, Jack?"
"The same," Jack said.
Janet said nervously, "I just wonder why you're asking these questions."
"Because," I explained, "it's amazing how many cases we've discovered where people have accidentally brought spirits into their houses by their interest in supernatural rites.
"For instance, we knew of a twenty-five-year-old woman who had a doll that was moving around by itself. The woman made the mistake of calling in a medium for a séance. During the séance

a spirit spoke and said it was the ghost of a dead little girl, and it asked for permission to reside in the doll. The doll's owner gave the spirit permission. But in the days that followed she began to very much regret what she'd done because the doll tried to possess people in the house, and even clawed and cut one person. The spirit was finally exorcised from the house when an Episcopal priest performed an exorcism.

"What happened is that the doll's owner made some major errors. She gave the spirit 'recognition' and then she gave it 'permission' to come into the house."

Lorraine shared another story with the Smurls that afternoon. "There was this very attractive, very intelligent nineteen-year-old woman who liked to 'dabble' in anything that gave her kicks. One day she bought a Ouija board and began playing with it. Then suddenly she found herself communicating with a spirit that managed to flatter the young woman into letting it come into her home. As usual, at first the spirit was a polite house guest and the young woman was thrilled that through the Ouija board she'd discovered the ultimate 'kick.'

"But very abruptly things changed. The spirit started fires, rampaged through rooms, and tried to physically harm the young woman's family. Finally, a Catholic priest we know had to be called in to perform an exorcism and ultimately the spirit was driven out."

"That's why it's so important," I explained, "not to 'dabble' in the black arts. And that's why we have to ask these questions."

Then I turned to Lorraine and said, "While I'm completing the interview, why don't you two take a tour of the house?"

Lorraine and Rosemary's combined psychic abilities are formidable enough one at a time; together they can turn up amazing truths no other process seems able to.

While Lorraine and Rosemary excused themselves, I went back to completing our profile of the Smurl family.

A Violent Spirit

*O*n the way up the stairs, Rose-
mary paused and closed her eyes and held her fingertips to her
head.

"My lord," she said.

Lorraine, preceding her friend up the stairs, turned around.
She knew what Rosemary was responding to. She had already
sensed it, too. The unmistakable air of evil that lay like a gray pall
over the entire house.

Rosemary put a hand to her chest, tried for a kind of half grin.
"You know what?"

"What?"

"I'm scared. I didn't think I would be but—"

Lorraine touched Rosemary's arm. "It's all right. We get
scared, too."

"You and Ed?"

Lorraine nodded. "It never gets easy, Rosemary." Then she
smiled. "Unfortunately."

* * *

"Did you hear something?" Rosemary asked.

"I—think so. I'm not sure."

Rosemary's fingers trembled. "I was sure I did."

They stood outside the last bedroom. The door was closed. All the other rooms had been checked out and found to be empty.

But a few moments earlier, coming down the hall, there had been a noise in this room, beyond the door.

"Well, we may as well go in," Lorraine said.

"Yes, may as well," Rosemary said, though she did not sound too sure of what she was doing.

Lorraine extended her hand. Turned the knob. Eased the door open.

A sweet-smelling sachet was on the air, as were the rich scents of other cosmetics. Late afternoon light cast long shadows across the wide double bed and the bureau. The wood in the old house creaked in the heart-pounding silence.

Lorraine stepped across the threshold, keeping her eyes moving for sight of anything suspicious. Her sensitivity as a psychic allows her to see the merest traces of the spirit world.

Rosemary followed Lorraine into the room, keeping close. Lorraine knelt down by the bed, lifted the colorful comforter and looked under it with a flashlight she kept in the pocket of her jacket. Nothing.

Next she looked behind a straight-backed chair and then behind the bureau. Still nothing.

There was only one place left and Rosemary had been staring at it anxiously for several minutes. The closet.

"Are we going to look inside?" Rosemary said.

"Yes. I've got a suspicion we'll find something there. I'm not even sure why."

With that, Lorraine moved to the closet door, steadied herself, and then flung it wide open, pushing the stark yellow beam of her flashlight inside immediately.

As the two women peered into the gloom of the closet, Lorraine's heart seemed to be lodged somewhere in her throat and a fine sheen of perspiration appeared on her forehead.

No matter how many times you encounter the satanic underworld, it is always frightening.

"Smell it?"

"Yes," Rosemary said. "Demons."

"The fourth one."

"And the worst one."

Lorraine stood completely still now and forced her eyes closed so tightly a headache threatened.

One of her psychic gifts was the ability to picture the invisible spirits that had infested a house.

Rosemary watched her. "Are you getting any sort of reading?"

Lorraine was. "I'm afraid for them," she said in a troubled voice.

"What do you see?"

Previously they had discovered three spirits in the house and had psychic profiles of them. One of them had been angry but with prayer and perseverance could be handled. This fourth one, however, was another matter.

"A demon," Lorraine said softly. "A genuine one." When she spoke at these times, her voice had the slightly dulled quality of someone in a trance.

"Do you think that's the one that's causing the problems?"

Lorraine, still trapped inside her psychic vision, nodded.

Rosemary blessed herself and then said a quick prayer that Lorraine would not be overwhelmed by the image filling her mind.

They were standing in the center of a tidy middle-class bedroom, dusk streaking the window, the scent of perfume and cigarette smoke on the air. This was not the sort of scene in which one should find evidence of Satan.

By now there could be no doubt.

It was ready for battle. Tireless battle. Which meant the Smurls would have to be ready to fight back if they were to survive.

Lorraine's eyes opened.

Rosemary said, "I hate to give them the news."

"If we don't, then they won't have a chance at driving him out."

"I know," Rosemary said softly. "It's just—"

"We'll have to help them, Rosemary. We'll have to help them every way we can."

The women said another prayer and then went downstairs to give the Smurls some very bad news.

Satan and His
Allies

*W*hen they were gathered at the
kitchen table, Janet having served fresh coffee and some sandwiches, Lorraine said, "There are four spirits in your home."

Janet and Jack glanced at each other uneasily.

"One of them is an elderly woman, probably senile, but not
violent. She's just confused. There's another woman, much
younger, and she's an insane, violent spirit who might want to
harm you, but I think she can be dealt with through prayer.

"The third spirit in the house is a man, and at this point all
we know about him is that he has a mustache and possesses the
ability to carry out great harm.

"Then there is the fourth spirit."

Here she paused. "I want you to remain calm when I tell you
about him."

Lorraine could see Janet and Jack tense.

"You're going to tell us it's a demon, aren't you?" Janet asked.

From her reading, she'd learned that sometimes spirit habitations could be relatively harmless, and often could be dispelled by constant prayer and house blessing.

Then there were demons.

Lorraine said, "The demon is here to create chaos and destroy the family."

She watched how Jack's open hand became a fist.

"The demon will use the other three spirits to his advantage," Lorraine went on. "It will appear in many guises and the way he will try to destroy you will assume many forms."

Jack's fist came down on the table. In his face you could see the weariness that frustration and useless rage had wrought. "But why would it pick on us?"

Now it was Ed's turn to speak. A big man with graying hair and piercing green eyes, he spread wide hands over the table and said, "It's like I said before, Jack, I suspect that the demon has been in the house—dormant—for decades. That I can't be sure of. But one thing I know is that your girls reaching puberty gave the demon energy. That's the classical pattern—puberty often brings on infestations. The demon is drawing on their emotional turbulence and now it's tapping into yours. You're like a battery it draws on for power. It's a real psychic explosion. It wants to keep you and your family confused and afraid; that's why it often appears to only one of you at a time. Nothing causes confusion the way that does. Carin says she sees something but nobody else sees it, so in the back of your mind, you wonder if Carin *really* saw anything. This is one way the demon has of keeping your family in constant turmoil, and trying to break you apart."

Jack sighed, lit a cigarette. "I can't sleep any more. I'm so tired, I could barely light this up." He waved the cigarette in Ed's direction.

"Remember what I said about you being a battery the demon draws power from? That's what's going on here. You're always tired and that's one reason you're always cold." Ed had a sip of coffee. "There's an entity that's trying to drain the life force from you."

Janet: "As we listened to the Warrens and Rosemary talk, I remember feeling a strange combination of relief and dread. The relief stemmed from the fact that it was reassuring somehow that somebody knew all these things about demonic infestation. We felt they could genuinely help us in our battle.

"The dread came from knowing that Ed and Lorraine and Rosemary were confirming our worst suspicions. Our house had been taken over by a demon."

An Experiment

*T*hat day Ed and Lorraine spent an hour with John and Mary Smurl, during which John admitted that he'd first been skeptical about the haunting at the duplex but now he knew better. "My God, Ed," Mary Smurl said, "you have to see what's going on here to believe it. I hope to God you believe us."

Ed smiled and touched Mary's hand. "We've seen the supernatural at work, Mary, and we're here to help."

Mary, still in failing health, smiled for the first time in weeks.

Around 6:30 Janet served a dinner of ham, potato salad, baked beans, and coffee.

During dinner, Ed said, "I'm going to have to ask you to trust me."

Jack said, "I think I can speak for both of us when I say that we do trust you."

Janet nodded.

"Then after we finish eating, why don't we go up to your bedroom."

Janet laughed. "Do we get a hint or are you going to keep us in suspense?"

Lorraine said, "It's a very special process. We're going to see if we can get the demon to expose itself in some way. Rosemary operates a camera with infrared film and I run a tape recorder. Sometimes we can record evidence of them." Ed glanced around the table at everybody. "Whenever you're ready. . . ."

In the bedroom, Jack, Janet, and Lorraine sat on the bed. Ed stood in a corner near the window. Rosemary positioned herself in front of the dresser. She operated a 35-mm camera on a tripod.

The room was long with the shadows of a winter night and the skeletal fingers of trees silhouetted by a streetlight outside. Bedsprings squeaked. Jack's breathing, from his heavy smoking, came hard.

Janet took her husband's hand, whispered, "I'm scared, hon."

Jack offered her a small smile and whispered back, "So am I."

"Now we need to pray," Ed said from the darkness in the corner.

Janet had always liked the resonant way prayer sounded in churches when many people prayed together. The room had that same feeling now as they all said three Our Fathers and three Hail Marys.

When the prayers were finished, Ed reached over and put a tape in the recorder. The beautiful strains of "Ave Maria" sung by a nun filled the room. The voice magnificent, the lyrics touching, the room seemed to be transformed for those long minutes. It felt friendly and peaceful again, the way it had when the Smurls had first moved here.

When the song had ended, Jack switched off the recorder and turned on the lights. To Lorraine, he said, "Anything?"

"Maybe."

"Can you describe it?"

She closed her eyes, touched long fingers to her forehead. "A very bright light in front of the closet and a dimmer one by the bedroom door."

Ed nodded. "We're going to do it again everybody. Ready?"

Jack and Janet nodded.

Once more, the lights went out and "Ave Maria" was played.

They had just begun to pray when they heard a tearing sound, as if something was being ripped from the wall.

"The mirror!" Janet said.

In the gloom they could see one of two large mirrors attached to the dresser with screws starting to move back and forth, as if it were going to rip free of its mountings.

"What is it?" Janet said.

"The demon," Ed replied calmly.

"Look at the TV!" Jack said.

The Smurls kept a black and white portable television set on their dresser. Lately the plug had given them some trouble so they now kept it unplugged except when in use, fearing fire.

But now an eerie white glow, the white silver color of apparitions, filled the screen and bathed Jack's and Janet's bodies in its strange color.

"I'd move away from there," Lorraine said. Then, hearing a crashing sound, she saw Rosemary jumping away from the dresser by which she'd been standing.

There was a rustling in the drawers now; before long they started to shake furiously.

Ed said, "I have to move quickly now."

The glow from the TV continued, as did the rustling inside the drawers. The mirror was shaking wildly, looking as if it were about to be torn completely free of the bureau.

Ed took a container of holy water, made a large sign of the cross in the air, and began sprinkling the room as he prayed. "In the name of Jesus Christ, I command you to be gone."

Janet and Jack held hands and stood very close together as Ed walked around with the holy water. He continued to pray.

Gradually, the glow from the TV diminished, and then was gone. Gradually, the bureau drawers ceased their violent rattling. Gradually, the mirror settled quietly back in place and remained stationary.

"The Lord be praised," Ed said, finally. "Let us offer our thanks."

Standing there in the shadows, they all said prayers of thanks.

Jack recalled later, "I had a sense at that moment that things were pretty much over, that Ed and Lorraine and Rosemary had pretty much figured out how to deal with the spirits that had invaded our house. But as Ed told us before they left, this was really just the beginning in a lot of ways. And unfortunately, his prediction turned out to be true."

Making Plans

*O*nce again, the Warrens, Rose-
mary, and the Smurls gathered around the kitchen table.

"In our investigations," Ed explained, "we've discovered that
there are 'hot spots' in houses that are haunted, places where we
pick up the strongest feeling of the spirits. Here, this means your
bedroom—it's really a haven for them. And to pass over into John
and Mary's duplex, they use the closet in your bedroom."

Jack: "As I sat in our living room, the windows dark with
night and frost collecting in their corners, I thought of how much
my life had changed in the past year, and now it was about to
change even more because we knew for sure what we were facing.
A part of what I felt, of course, was fear that if anybody found out
about what was really going on here they'd think my family was
either making these things up or that we were crazy."

"How can we fight them?" Janet asked.

"You can start with this," Ed said, and handed her a piece of paper. A prayer had been typed on it: "In the name of Jesus Christ, in the blood of Christ, I command you to leave and to return from where you came."

Ed said, "Use this when you feel in danger. If you can, use holy water and make a large sign of the cross, too."

"And tomorrow," Lorraine said, "there are some things you should get."

Rosemary nodded. "We'd advise that you go to a church diocesan shop and buy religious candles and incense and get plenty of holy water."

Ed finished his coffee. "One more thing. I'd really urge you to call a priest tomorrow and see if he would consider doing an exorcism here."

"Will they do that?" Janet asked.

"If you convince them that this is really happening," Ed said.

"I'll call the parish first thing in the morning," Janet said.

Jack sighed, stubbed out his cigarette. He looked evenly at Ed Warren and said, "I want to ask you a simple question."

"Sure."

"Is all this going to help?"

"I'm going to give you a simple answer," Ed said. "I don't know. The demon we're dealing with here is very strong. Very strong. Sometimes we are able to drive these things out through fairly easy tactics." He shook his head. "Other times—"

He did not have to finish the sentence.

Lorraine said, "What we've done here tonight may just be the preliminary work. We'll call you in the morning and see how things are going. We may have to send over a special team to keep helping you."

"You'd do that?" Janet said.

Lorraine smiled. "That's why we're here, Janet, to help."

"But we couldn't afford—"

Lorraine raised her hand. "We don't charge for our services. We've had three books written about us, we've been consultants to Dino DeLaurentis, and we're constantly on the lecture circuit.

Fortunately, that enables us to provide our services free of charge."

She patted Janet's hand then glanced at the watch on her slender wrist. "It's time we go. We've got a long drive ahead of us."

At the door, Janet said, "We really can't thank you enough."

"Just remember about going to the church store tomorrow. And keep that prayer with you at all times," Ed said. Then he looked at the four Smurl children, who had been sitting in the front room watching television as the grown-ups discussed the infestation. He smiled and waved to them. "And remember, girls, make sure your parents stay just as brave as you are!"

The girls laughed.

The Warrens headed out to their van in the snowy, bitter cold night.

A Night of Trial

*A*fter the Warrens and Rosemary left, Janet and Jack sat in the living room with their four girls and explained to them the events of the day.

"What are we going to do?" Heather, the second eldest, asked after her mother finished talking.

Janet explained how tomorrow they were going to go to the church store and buy various things. "And we're going to have to pray harder than we ever have."

Jack put out his hands. Shannon, one of the twins, took one of his hands, Dawn the other. Then Janet and Heather and Carin joined their hands, too.

For the next twenty minutes, the Smurl family prayed with an intensity it had never summoned before.

Evidence of an entity that could well destroy their entire family had been presented on this day.

Only God's help could save them.

As the girls were getting ready for bed—brushing their teeth, slipping into heavy cotton pajamas—Janet and Jack went into the kitchen.

"I don't want the girls to know this," Janet said, taking her husband's hand, "but I'm very scared."

"So am I."

"What are we going to do?"

"The only thing we can—what the Warrens told us to do."

She sighed. "Maybe it would be better if we all slept downstairs tonight."

Jack thought a moment. "I don't think so, honey."

"But why not?"

He squeezed her hand and gave her a soft, tender kiss. "We can beat this thing. And that's what we've got to remember. *We can beat this thing.*" He said this with the sort of angry determination he would more and more come to draw on in the ensuing months.

That night, the family took their usual places in the three bedrooms.

"Do you know the thing we saw one day?" Carin whispered.

The twins had been tucked into their beds, prayers said, lights off. But they were too stirred up from the day's events to sleep.

"The gray thing?" Shannon said.

"Yes."

"Do you think it's in our room right now?"

"Do you?"

"Are you just trying to scare me?"

"No."

"I don't think it's in here," Shannon said.

"Are you just saying that?"

"No."

They said nothing for a time. There were just the sounds of their own breathing and the winter wind rattling windows throughout the house.

For young children, shadows can be as deep and dark as the ocean. And that was how it seemed to Carin and Shannon as they lay in their beds, listening.

Then the knock came.

"Did you hear that?" Carin whispered.

"Yes."

From the beginning of the infestation, the Smurls had been bothered by knockings within the walls. Sometimes these were little more than single raps. Other times they were sharp, staccato bursts, as if a hammer were being pounded very rapidly against the wall.

There was a third variety, a deep, imploding sound that seemed to send tremors from the foundation of the house up through the floors and all the way to the chimney. The Smurls sensed that an earthquake might sound and feel like this.

It was this thunderous sound that caused the girls to sit up now.

"Something's weird," Carin said.

"I know," Shannon said softly.

"You afraid?"

"Ummmm."

Carin sighed. "You think everything's going to be all right?"

Shannon didn't have any answer for that one.

In the bedroom of Jack and Janet: "What was that?"

The stinging slap had sounded like leather against flesh.

"It just hit me," Janet said.

Then there was another slapping sound and Janet cried out. Jack grabbed her.

There in the darkness of their bedroom, he felt forces swirling around them, like a vortex that would take them down, down, into a deep and unimaginable hell.

He clung to his wife as if she were drowning.

Then he felt a tickling sensation on the bottoms of his feet.

Not the sort of tickling that causes laughter but the sort that can induce weakness and even madness if prolonged enough.

Jack jumped around on the bed as if he were losing his mind.

"Jack, Jack!" Janet cried, as invisible hands continued to slap at her and now to produce an ugly animal frenzy in her husband.

Then the knocking began.

The deep, cavernous knocking that reverberated throughout the house.

Boom.

Boom.

Boom.

"They want to prove to us they're the superior ones," Janet said.

And as if to confirm her words, at that instant their portable television set bloomed again with the eerie, pale glow it had emitted when the Warrens had been in here.

The glow grew so intense this time that Jack and Janet had to look away in pain.

The set was still disconnected.

Jack flung himself off the bed and stood bare-chested, his hands big fists.

"Why don't you show yourself to us so we can have a fair fight?" he shouted at the shifting shadows.

Janet came to his side, clung to him.

It took her many minutes to calm her husband down.

The knocking in the walls continued.

It was like being on military patrol.

The good German shepherd patrolled the hall in front of the girls' rooms, keeping alert in case he needed to warn the girls of anything. By now, Simon was well aware in his way of demons and what they could do to animals of all description, human and otherwise.

Simon was joined throughout the night by Jack Smurl. Carrying a flashlight long and heavy enough to double as a formidable weapon, Jack woke many times during the long night to go in and check on his girls.

He knew they'd heard the knocking in the walls and he'd gone in to comfort them when the sounds became especially bad.

Finally, around 3:00 A.M., the pounding ceased.

But Jack, frightened for the sake of his girls, took no chances.

He still woke, he still patrolled. In the morning he was, of course, exhausted.

As he was eating breakfast, the phone rang and Janet answered it.

"Hello?" she said.

"Hi, this is Ed Warren. We're just checking on how things went last night."

Janet sighed, eyed Jack nervously. "Why don't I let you talk to Jack, Ed?"

"Sure. Put him on."

Jack came to the phone and explained what had happened during the night.

"I was afraid something like this might happen," Ed said thoughtfully on the other end. "They're not going to give up. At least not without a real battle."

"We're going to call a priest today."

"And be sure to get those religious articles."

"Absolutely."

"And keep angry. Don't give in to them. We've already talked about recognizing them in various ways, giving them dominance over you and letting them use your energy. Well, anger is one way of making sure that you don't give up."

Jack said, in a low voice so the girls eating their Cream of Wheat couldn't hear, "My family looks like a bunch of zombies this morning. This place was like living in a bunker last night. Like there's a war going on."

Ed Warren said softly, "Jack, I've got to be honest with you."

"Honest about what?"

Ed paused. "Jack, there *is* a war going on."

An Indifferent Cleric

Janet: "We'd always counted on help from the church. But we found out—bitterly, I have to say— that this wasn't going to be the case.

"One of the days Ed and Lorraine were here, Lorraine called our local parish and explained to one of the priests—a Father Costigan—what was going on in our house and said that we needed help. He was very curt with her, saying he was busy with a wedding rehearsal, and that she should call another time. After he'd hung up, Lorraine said they were used to this kind of treatment from priests.

"Ed then suggested that we get certain religious objects and have them blessed for the safety of our family. But when I went to get them blessed, the same priest treated me basically the way he'd treated Lorraine. Even though I told him about everything that had been happening to us, he showed no real interest or sympathy.

"He blessed the objects I'd brought but he didn't use holy water and as soon as he was done, he rushed away. He didn't ask me any questions at all."

This was to be only the beginning of Janet's problems with the church she'd grown up trusting and believing in.

The Demon Stirs

*I*n the days following Father Costigan's refusal to visit the Smurl home, and the depressing impact this refusal had on the family, the Smurls discovered just how accurate Ed Warren had been about their being involved in "a war."

A Discovery

After school one day, Dawn came home to find her makeup missing from her bureau. This was typical of events around the house lately—the spirits "vanishing" many of the family's belongings.

On this particular afternoon, however, Dawn did not react in the way an average sixteen-year-old would when presented with evidence of demons. Instead, she got angry. She even joked about it.

"I know why you took my makeup!" she shouted to the spirits she felt in the room. "It's because you're ugly and your mommy dresses you funny!"

Janet, passing by her daughter's bedroom, heard this and began laughing.

She stopped laughing when violent banging began inside the walls. Now Janet became apprehensive. Had Dawn made the demon so angry that it would hurt her?

Janet had promised herself that the next time the wall-poundings began, she would run and get a tape recorder, which she did now.

Kneeling by the knocking, Janet started the tape recorder and then said, "I want to communicate with you."

"Mother!" Dawn whispered.

Addressing the demon again, Janet said, "I want you to knock once for yes and twice for no. Do you understand?

Dawn went over and sat on the bed, both afraid and fascinated.

"Do you understand?" Janet repeated to the demon.
Nothing.

Janet checked the tape recorder and then proceeded to have a most curious conversation.

"Are you here to harm us?"
Nothing.
"It's not going to talk to us," Dawn said.
"Are you here to harm us?" Janet repeated.
This time there came a knock.
A single knock.
The answer was yes.
The demon was here to harm them.
Janet gasped.

"Are you here to harm me?" Janet asked, wanting to make sure that the first knock had indeed been in response to her question.

Another single knock.

Yes.

Janet knew that her next question might cause the demon to go berserk. She would introduce into the conversation the name of the being that had driven Satan from heaven: God himself.

Janet said, "Do you believe in Jesus Christ?"

The response was immediate and furious.

The banging became so loud and intense that Janet was pushed back from the wall, kicking over the tape recorder as she was flung over it.

Dawn buried her face in the pillow, trying to shield her ears from the overwhelming rapping.

"Stop! Stop!" Janet called out to the demon.

Three or four minutes later, the banging stopped.

Janet's first move was to right the recorder, rewind the tape, and play it back to see if the entire episode had been recorded. Thankfully, it had been.

She went over and sat on the bed next to Dawn. Sliding her arm around her, "Why didn't you run out of the room, honey? I know you were scared."

Dawn grinned. "I wanted to be here in case I needed to protect you."

Janet had never been prouder of her daughter than at that moment.

BATHING TROUBLE

Finished with her housework for the day, Janet Smurl was taking a bath.

She'd just gotten settled in the tub, lathering herself with Dove, when suddenly she felt eyes on her.

She had never felt quite so naked or vulnerable.

She continued with her bath, soaping her face gently and rinsing off the soap right away.

Then the whistling began.

It was the kind of lascivious whistling women have to endure around groups of drunken men, filled with both innuendo and threat.

Janet began screaming.

Jack, reading the paper downstairs, ran up the stairs two at a time. He flung back the bathroom door and came in to find Janet crouched in the corner of the tub, trembling.

"It's in here!" she said.

Then she told him about the whistling.

"Please stay here with me, Jack. Please."

"Don't worry," Jack said.

Across from the bathroom door was a crucifix he'd used to keep the hallway safe. He pushed the door wide open now so that Janet could see the cross.

He sat in there with her until she finished her bath.

As she toweled off, Janet said dejectedly, "Now it's getting so bad we need a bodyguard to take a bath."

STRANGE WOMEN

Exhausted from a long day at work, and from the tension that filled the house, Jack fell asleep one Friday night earlier than usual.

Around 2 A.M. he was awakened by the sounds of people talking. He thought it might be the twins. But at 2:00 A.M.?

Then he looked up and saw two women in the room. One appeared to be in her early forties, the other around twenty. They wore old-fashioned bonnets and long dresses that cast an eerie sheen similar to that of the glowing TV set. Oddly, their hair had no exact color.

Then they were gone.

Instantly.

In the morning, Jack told Janet about the peculiar apparition. They both agreed that it could well have been a dream brought on by the stress the family was under.

That night, however, the same two women reappeared.

Jack watched them as they stood in the shadowy corner of the bedroom. He tried to wake Janet but couldn't (by now he knew that she was experiencing the "psychic sleep" that allowed the demon to appear to one person without having the other person awaken to corroborate the appearance).

This night the women began whispering to each other. Then the younger one turned to Jack and smiled. Her lips curled sarcastically.

He tried to cry out but found he had no voice.

He tried to move off the bed but found he was paralyzed.

He tried to wake Janet again but to no avail.

He lay and watched them whisper and sneer at him.

Then they eased back into the closet from where they'd come and disappeared.

Even three full days and nights later, Jack still shuddered involuntarily whenever he thought of the two women and their strangely threatening presence.

The Team Arrives

*E*d and Lorraine Warren began, by early February, to call the Smurls virtually every day. The assault by the demon grew worse daily.

Finally, the Warrens dispatched to the Smurls' home a team of psychic researchers who were to analyze the family's situation in the smallest detail.

On an overcast February morning, a dark sedan pulled up in front of the Smurls' duplex, carrying Charles Cravatas and Tony Clericuzio. Charles was a licensed practical nurse from Bridgeport, Connecticut, who had assisted the Warrens in many dealings with the supernatural. Tony is from Huntington and presently studies demonology with the Warrens.

Charles: "As Ed had warned me, I could sense a demonic presence even from across the street. I looked around at the pleasant houses lining both sides of the street, at the everyday sights of children in bulky snowsuits playing behind mounds of snow, and at dogs and cats hurrying down the street through the cold, and

I was amazed as I always am that in the most common of settings, such as this one, Satan finds a way to enter people's lives."

After meeting Janet, Jack, and the children, Charlie and Tony began setting up tape recorders in the upstairs hallway, examining the "entrance points" the spirits used to go back and forth between the duplexes, and interviewing each member of the Smurl family.

"I want to tell you something right up front," Charles said when they'd all gathered in the living room. "I'm going to start with the assumption that you're not telling us the truth."

"*What?*" Janet said, somewhat shocked and insulted.

"You're going to need to *prove* to me that your house has been infested."

"But why?"

"Because many people do things like this to get attention for themselves or just to play a kind of practical joke."

"But after all we've been through—" Janet said.

Charles held up his hand. "I've been told you've been through all these things but I don't know that for a fact."

"Now wait a minute—" Jack spoke up.

Charles said, "Put yourself in my place, Jack. I'm a trained psychic investigator. If I just automatically accepted everybody's word for things, would I really be doing my job?"

"The Warrens said you'd ask us some tough questions," Janet said, laughing and easing the tension in the room. "They sure weren't kidding."

Over the next few hours, the Smurls relived the entire haunting, though as Janet admitted, "We're not sure when it started exactly. I guess we'd have to date it—to be official—about the time that both Mary and I saw the black form." The Smurls then went on to detail all the major rappings, odors, whispers, and apparitions that had been inflicted on them, concluding with the appearance of the strange women in Janet's and Jack's bedroom.

"You didn't find anything in the morning?" Charles asked Jack.

"Find anything?"

"Any evidence."

"Like what?"

"Oh, a button. A strand of their oddly colored hair, maybe."

"No."

"But you're sure you didn't dream them?"

"Now wait a minute—"

Janet gently patted Jack's hand. He calmed down. "I know I didn't dream them. They were too real. Everything about it was real."

Charles nodded, made notes in the thick book lying open on his lap.

Tony: "He was questioning them about the two women when I heard the first knocking. It was incredible—and really frightening. I'd been studying demonology with the Warrens for some time but I'd never actually had this type of experience before. It was like the air in the room froze. Charles ran upstairs to make sure the recorders were working properly so we'd be sure to get the rappings on the tape."

For the next hour, hard rapping ranged from room to room as the spirits seemed to work themselves up into a kind of frenzy.

Charles: "By then, of course, I didn't have any doubt what we were dealing with. It was demonic infestation. We spent the entire night listening to, recording, and cataloguing a variety of experiences associated with the supernatural, everything from tape recordings on which we can hear the rappings to odors that appeared in certain places in the house. We made entries in our logs every five minutes. By morning, we were all exhausted. Janet made us a great breakfast of eggs and sausage and toast and then we went back to Connecticut to talk with the Warrens. We had several tapes that we felt proved conclusively that a demon was in the house."

Another member of the team, Mike Kessel, joined Tony on the next trip.

Mike interviewed Lenora Brinser and her parents across the street, and then picked up with the Smurls where Charles had left off, asking them if they believed in ghosts, if they had any unusual religious affiliations, or if they had done anything that might have invited the demon in.

Midway through Mike's visit the pounding began again.

Mike: "You try to describe it to people and they can't imagine it. You're standing looking at a plain wall and all of a sudden these sounds erupt from inside, as if somebody is running up and down the wall, somebody invisible. It gives you chills. It really does.

"But the rapping wasn't the only thing that bothered me that afternoon. It was the look of the family. I work as a life-support technician for a commercial ambulance service and I'm also a certified evidence technician. I see people under very stressful circumstances. By the way the Smurls behaved, I could see that they were being pushed to the brink. I could see that we—meaning the entire Warren team—were going to have to get involved."

Next day, following a long meeting in the morning, Ed and Lorraine Warren decided on two things—to pay the Smurls a second visit, and to get various other experts involved.

The people they selected included a doctor who is a medical examiner in Connecticut; Roger Coyle, a seventeen-year veteran of the Bristol, Connecticut police department; Al Voghel, who designs data-communication networks for a large insurance company; and Chris McKinnell, the Warrens' grandson, who has a BA in psychology. At different times over the ensuing months these people played key roles in trying to drive the spirits from the duplex on West Chase Street.

At the moment, however, the Warrens' presence was required and so on a sunny March day they again made the four-hour drive. By now, they knew much more about the nature of the infestation.

Unfortunately, most of their news for the Smurls would be bad news.

THE APPRENTICE DEMONOLOGIST:

The odd thing is, as a boy he was never interested in comic books, or movies, or paperbacks about the occult. A straight-A student who preferred history to English and math to music, he was one of those "sensible" young men who came dangerously close to being a "nerd." Today he laughs: "I had all the usual teenage failings, the zits, the wrinkled clothes, the anxiety around pretty girls, the indecision about my future. But if nothing else, I was 'realistic.' My parents always praised me for that—I had a part-time job at a small grocery store when I was eleven and ever since then I've worked steadily. I always took care of the things they bought me—the Schwinn I got for my tenth birthday looks almost as good today as it did when my parents gave it to me for Christmas fifteen years ago—and I was always in on time and always told them what I was going to do. About the only 'big night' I ever had in high school was once when a friend of mine and I took four cans of Budweiser from his dad's refrigerator and sat out in the garage and drank them. This was at the same time, socially, when most kids our age were smoking pot or taking LSD. And this kind of conservatism extended into my college years, too. I decided to be an engineer. Nice, safe, secure, and empirical. I wasn't religious and whenever anybody mentioned any sort of weird phenomena—and by that I include everything from demons to UFOs—I laughed my engineer laugh and dismissed it. I remember seeing one of my real idols, Arthur C. Clarke, on a TV show once wondering aloud why UFOs, for example, never landed where large numbers of people could see them? He then went on to disprove—at least to my satisfaction—every single famous incident of a saucer sighting."

David remained just as skeptical as he'd been during his college years. By the time he graduated, he found that the job market he'd taken for granted had shrunk considerably. He spent hours a day in job interviews but to no avail. "It was really depressing. I couldn't even get entry-level work. This was right at the top of the recession. I just took what I could find, usually whatever the local state employment office could find for me on a day-work basis. I lived at home, of course, because I couldn't afford to move out and find my own apartment."

One cold Friday night in November, bored and depressed that his birthday was coming up and that there was still no job prospect in sight, David went to the Regal, a relic of the era when movie theaters had been built to resemble palaces, and saw The Amityville Horror.

David: "Ordinarily, I wouldn't have chosen a movie like that. For entertainment I liked Clint Eastwood or Charles Bronson. I still hadn't developed any special taste for horror or the occult. I didn't even like science fiction. But that Friday night I needed to get out of the house—I'd just spent all day unloading crates in a discount warehouse—and Amityville was the only movie that looked even vaguely interesting. I'd read a few things about the incident and I suppose that was why I was at least a little intrigued by it."

The odd thing was, David recounted later, he didn't care much for the movie, thinking it was overacted and illogical in several places. But: *"It did trigger something in me. For the first time I wondered if all my skepticism about occult phenomena wasn't a bit too pat. Maybe I'd closed my eyes to a whole lot of things."*

On Monday, David went to the state employment office only to find that they didn't even have any day work for him. It was another bitterly cold day, and having a twenty-five minute wait ahead of him for a city bus, David walked two blocks to a branch library where he went, as usual, to the nonfiction section.

Ordinarily, David's reading ran to books on astronomy and current debate on scientific issues.

The Amityville Horror *still fresh in his mind, today David picked up a formidable new volume entitled* Mysteries *by Colin Wilson, which he opened at random. The first paragraph he read was on page 486: "But ever since Dr. Rhodes Buchanan began testing the students of the Cincinnati Medical School for psychometric powers in the 1840s, modern researchers have realized that such powers are far commoner than we think. . . . Poltergeist experiences occur every day of the week; investigators like Hans Bender and William Roll have examined hundreds."*

David spent the next six hours in the library—scarcely aware of afternoon becoming dusk—poring over every single word the author had to say on the subject of the paranormal and the occult.

Absolutely without planning it—and even to a degree fighting his better instincts—David Wilson, became, that afternoon, a fledgling demonologist.

Lorraine Shares Some Disturbing Facts

"**P**lease don't be afraid of what we're going to explain to you," Lorraine said to the Smurls next afternoon as the family and the Warrens gathered in the living room. She opened her large, leatherbound notebook and began to read.

In summary, she told them that the investigation revealed that all the classic signs of infestation were present in the Smurl duplex with one exception. "You're a very solid family and that's what's so unusual. But that's why I feel so much hope that we can deal with this very well. Because you've got the right kind of spiritual reserves to draw on."

She then went on to list the incidents the Smurls had related to the investigating team as further proof of infestation, finally concentrating on the black form. "This is the demon. It never stands erect, it always hunches over when it walks or stands, and it can appear out of nowhere. It can disappear into a closet or wall or anywhere it wants to go. It can also bring a very powerful telepathic hypnosis to bear on any human mind." She nodded to Ed. "We knew a woman once who swore to us that she'd seen the room she was in go up in flames—literally explode. But that hadn't really happened, of course. It was just the demon playing tricks with her mind and trying to confuse her. The demon counts on that—on its power to confuse people. That's its greatest weapon."

Lorraine went on to explain that the spirits roam the earth because they have not accepted the death of their physical bodies. Most spirits don't harm people but they "can be used by demons, as in your house, to become malevolent."

Then Janet asked about all the things that had been missing from the house—clothing, books, makeup, jewelry, and the rosary.

Ed explained that this kind of activity was common in hauntings, another way that the demon confused people and caused trouble in the family. He said, "Remember how you told us that Dawn and Shannon got into an argument because Dawn thought that Shannon had taken something of hers? That's a good example of what the demon likes to do."

As they talked, Lorraine glanced out the window and saw a yellow school bus working its way down the street. "I'd like to wrap this up before the kids get home, so I'll be brief." She pointed to her notebook. "I've looked over the notes the entire team took and I'd have to say that this demon is even worse than we suspected."

She gave Janet time to put her head down in her hands and shake her head. Obviously Janet felt both bitter and weary. Lorraine was used to seeing these emotions reflected on the haggard faces of a demon's victims.

Lorraine said, "And this morning I experienced the demon firsthand myself."

Janet's head came up. "You did?"

"Unfortunately, yes. Right after we got here, I went upstairs and started walking around the girls' rooms. When I was near Dawn's bed, I heard scratching sounds on the window. It sounded like something frantically clawing at the glass. When I looked up I saw the black form standing outside, looking in. It was really hideous."

Ed, trying to reassure the Smurls, said, "We've found a priest to bless the house."

"A priest? Really?" Janet smiled for the first time that day.

Ed frowned. "Since you don't seem to be having much luck with the church, we thought we'd try."

Lorraine said, "We just hope it will do some good."

The priest came promptly at 6:00 P.M.

He was a calm, courteous man and Janet liked him, though she noticed how apprehensive he looked, and his furtive glances at Jack and herself made her feel like some kind of freak.

Had the priest heard stories about the Smurls?

Was the word getting around that the family was crazy?

Finished with his rituals, the priest bade them a quiet good night and left.

"He's heard about us, hasn't he?" Janet asked Ed once the priest had gone.

Ed was uncomfortable with her question, knowing what it implied. "He was probably just nervous."

"People are starting to talk about us, aren't they?" Janet said.

Ed sighed. "Possibly. Word gets around and people start to gossip."

"And the priest has heard some of that gossip."

Lorraine sighed. "She may be right, Ed. Maybe word has gotten all over the area."

"A priest," Janet said. "You'd think of all people, he'd want to be helpful." She thought again of how her church, the church she'd been a part of since her baptism, had deserted her.

She excused herself and went into the kitchen and wept soft, silent tears.

That night they all went out to eat in a local restaurant—the girls using the occasion to get their standard favorites: malts, cheeseburgers, and french fries (and Janet glad to see that even in the midst of all this craziness her daughters had not lost their appetites)—and then they returned to the house where Ed was going to perform the very dangerous rite of religious provocation.

At that moment they didn't have any idea just how dangerous it would prove to be.

ED WARREN:

After dinner that evening, I went up to Janet's and Jack's bedroom prepared to force the demon to expose itself through a ritual known as religious provocation.

It works this way: You invoke the name of Jesus Christ and his sacred blood and then you command the demon to reveal itself and be banished from the home.

In the past we'd often had success with this ritual and I was very hopeful that it would prove useful that night. But when I entered the bedroom, I felt a chill in the air, as if a presence were literally robbing the air of warmth, and I saw on the bed the shredded spread Janet had found clawed one morning.

I walked around the room, then paused over by the closet, which was, I knew, where the spirits resided, from which point they passed between duplexes.

And then my senses were overcome—I don't know any better way to describe it. Have you ever had anybody hold a vial of camphor up to your nose? Do you know how it seems to stun you and knock you backward?

That's what began to happen to me.

Then things got even worse: I started to say a prayer out loud and invisible fingers seized my throat, choking me.

I'd never been strangled before and the sensation was incredible, especially since I couldn't see my assailant. I could feel my lungs burning for air and I felt blood filling my face. I was hot and dizzy and unable to breathe.

When we'd investigated Amityville, I'd had an experience where I felt as if somebody had put a hot, steamy rag over my face, but this was much worse. I was literally pawing at the air like an animal.

I realized there was only one way I could save myself and that was to place myself into what is called religious resistance. It's very difficult to do at a time when you're being assaulted but it was my only hope.

As carefully as I could, I envisioned the white light of Jesus Christ around my body. I pictured my body glowing with this protective seal—literally the love of God.

Gradually, even though I was knocked back flat on the bed, I began to feel the unseen thumbs that pressed at my throat slowly begin to ease up.

At this point one of my assistants, Roger Coyle, came into the room and saw what was happening to me. He began praying with me and the pressure on my throat let up even more. Finally, I was able to sit up and breathe normally again.

Roger asked me many questions about what had happened and we both agreed that the infestation in this house was probably the worst we'd ever seen.

And what happened next certainly bore out this suspicion.

Despite the fact that the demon had attempted to strangle me, I planned to keep on performing religious provocation in each of the bedrooms, my hope being that in this way the Smurls would have some peace.

I stood in the hallway, gathering my senses and strength and my courage, still shaken from nearly being choked to death.

In one hand I carried a crucifix and, as it turned out, it was a good thing I had it.

The adjacent bedroom was shadowy. The beds were made, clothes neatly put away in the closet, books, records, and school items lining shelves.

I had just started to pray when I sensed an abrupt chill pass through the room like an invisible cloud. In less time than it took to say three Hail Marys, the room temperature dropped at least thirty degrees. I continued to demand—even though I was starting to get very cold—that the demon be gone.

Obviously it was not responding happily to my demands because I saw a thin, silver gossamer thread start to form in the ornate mirror above the bureau.

Stunned, I watched as the thread began to form letters of the alphabet—first Y and then an O and then a U.

I continued to shake from the freezing cold but I had no choice but to watch fascinated as the vile message began to show itself fully. Though I'd investigated hauntings for more than forty years now, I'd never seen anything at all like this.

Then the message was complete.

It read: "You filthy bastard. Get out of this house."

A horrible stench filled my nostrils.

The temperature fell even more and I felt a dangerous paralysis set in. Demons often like to immobilize people; it makes it much easier for them to work their tricks.

Then I remembered the crucifix in my hand. I raised it to the mirror and commanded the demon to leave. At first its message remained clear and in place but the longer I cried out Christ's name, the less vivid the gossamer writing was.

Finally, the threadlike material began to melt, almost like snow exposed to brilliant sunlight.

The stink left the room.

I felt my body temperature began to warm.

I wish I could say that I felt as if I'd just won a victory but I didn't.

Then, and not without guilt, I let my eyes fall to the crucifix in my hand. I thought of Christ and his suffering. What was my small ordeal compared to his?

A smile crossed my face as I stared at the place where the

mirror-message had appeared. I should take heart from what the Lord Jesus had just helped me do. I shouldn't feel fear.

Armed with new determination and after checking the last bedroom, I went downstairs to see what the others were doing.

THE APPRENTICE DEMONOLOGIST:

At the same time that Janet and Jack Smurl were just beginning to experience the first terrifying examples of demonic infestation, David Wilson was starting to look around for serious contacts in the world of the paranormal.

While his days were still spent looking for some way in which to put his engineering degree to use, he visited the library as often as he could, culling through books and newspapers that reached as far back as the last century.

Being both intelligent and healthily skeptical, David soon learned that there was a wide cavern separating the genuine students of the occult and those who were simply seeking thrills or publicity.

In his bedroom, the walls covered with posters of the rock group Heart ("Leave it to Cleavage" someone had once remarked by way of explaining the group's success), David spent hours nibbling on Fritos and drinking Diet Pepsi and poring over the books he'd brought home from the library.

Occasionally, when bitter winter wind whipped the windows, and when the hour was past midnight, he heard creaking in the house he'd never heard before. A sense of something sinister filled him at these moments and he would set his book down, his heart pounding, realizing that for all his deeply entrenched skepticism, he was very much afraid.

One time, when fear suddenly overcame him, he broke its spell by wondering how his parents would feel if their twenty-three-

year-old son came into their room and asked if he could sleep with them? The image was so hilarious that he set his book aside and took a break, going downstairs to have a sandwich and then went into the living room to watch one of the few science fiction movies he'd ever liked, It Came from Outer Space, *an especially convincing account of an alien invasion written by Ray Bradbury and directed by the great Jack Arnold.*

This was his life, then—useless job interview after useless job interview (he was sending out resumés in ever-widening patterns, all the way west to Chicago by now) and hours in the library or in his room reading books on the paranormal and the occult.

In a magazine he found the name of a group of local paranormalists who met three times a month. He spent the week before the meeting as excited as he'd been about his first (and, alas, last) date with Susan Kramer, only to find the group composed of people whom his father would describe as "kooks." It seemed as if everybody in the group had been kidnaped at least once by aliens and several seemed to have round-trip tickets to the solar system. Even if they were sincere, he found their tales (when matched against his skepticism) impossible to believe.

But over the course of these months he was becoming something of an alien himself. Unemployment does not do a whole lot for a person's self-esteem and the routine of filling out job applications gets not only demeaning but exhausting.

In his nightly prayers (he'd never lost the habit of praying, even if he didn't believe in the deity exactly as he/she/it was portrayed by organized religion) he asked for a job, a girlfriend, long good health for his parents, and some sort of sign that his sudden interest in the occult wasn't just some aberration brought on by the stress of not being able to find a job.

A few weeks later, at least one of his prayers was answered. In a branch library he'd never visited before, he found a thick hardback book called The Demonologist, *by a writer named Gerald Brittle.*

More than he could have ever imagined, the book he held would change David Wilson's life in the most profound way.

Peculiar Bites

*A*fter his own startling experi-
ence in the bedroom, Ed found that the team had had one of its
own. Al Voghel, who had been carrying a video pack on his back,
had felt his shoulders being jerked first one way and then another
by a force he could neither see nor explain.

Al also had the sensation that electricity was filling the air in
the room. The hair on his arms stood straight up.

Chris McKinnell, already an expert on demonology, knew
exactly what was going on. "One of the spirits is drawing its
energy from you. You're like a power plant for it."

Lorraine, who had come into the room, began praying for Al
and very soon the sensation of electricity surging through his body
left him.

They were most peculiar bite marks.

They had been inflicted on Jack Smurl a few days earlier
while he was in the shower.

At first he'd wondered if a wasp might not have gotten into the bathroom. Then he remembered the month. Wasps in February?

The next bite was so severe that Jack had cried out in pain.

Now Chris McKinnell was snapping photographs of a bite on Jack's ear.

"When he came down from the bathroom," Janet explained, "his whole left ear was red."

Ed Warren, watching as Chris snapped photographs for later evidence, said, "How many bite marks are there?"

"Three," Janet said.

"It's mocking the Trinity," Ed said. "Three of a kind is always symbolic of the mockery."

"Will it go away?" Janet said, still concerned that the bite might become a serious infection.

"I'm pretty sure it will," Ed said, "if we just keep on praying."

A few days later the bite had gone away entirely. But that was one of the few pieces of good news the Smurls had that week. Simon, their beloved dog, was levitated and in the process became so frightened that Janet and Jack wondered if a dog could be driven insane. And Mary Smurl once again saw the strange dark transparent form in her bedroom, standing in the doorway as if summoning her to some terrible fate.

LORRAINE WARREN:

When our grandson Chris McKinnell returned from an early spring visit to the Smurls, he, Ed, and I sat down for an in-depth assessment of the situation at the house, from the demonic rapping that plagued their nights to the psychological effects the infestation was having on the family. Chris found them to be incredibly resilient.

One aspect of their predicament ran consistent with the classic pattern: Demonic spirits are often attracted to houses where young girls are going through puberty. The spirits draw on the particular type of energy the girls emit, the emotional level being very high, and ideal for a spirit to feed on.

What didn't run to form was the fact that the Smurls were a happy, religious family. To be honest, many if not most of the families we investigate are anything but happy or religious. What we usually find is drug or alcohol abuse, adultery, even occasionally child abuse—each an ideal entry point for demonic spirits.

But here we had the most diabolical of demons—believe me, when a demon rips a light fixture from the ceiling and nearly kills a young girl with it, we are dealing with the most serious form of infestation—and this was happening to a family who had not invited the spirits in through occult means or through sinful lives. And we now had exhaustive evidence to prove this.

Chris and the team had spent long nights, entire weekends, and endless hours interviewing, evaluating, photographing, and recording family members and curious phenomena.

Certainly one of Chris's strangest revelations to us on that spring afternoon when we were doing our final assessment was the story Jack had related to him.

Simon, the family dog, had dematerialized right in front of Janet's eyes, and then, howling, had come back into earthly existence.

You can't gauge the horrible impact this must have had on a sensitive woman like Janet.

But even though the dematerialization was dramatic, it was probably no more impactful on the Smurls' mental state than the constant wall-banging, door-slamming, and whispering the spirits inflicted on the family. Our research teams keep their records in five-minute increments so it is possible for us to chart out the exact level of the infestation over long periods of time.

Based on the team's notes, and on Chris's articulate evaluation of the situation, we decided to move for a full exorcism of the Smurl home.

Because of two particularly terrible events, we just wish we'd moved sooner.

Raped
by a Succubus

Q. Jack, would you describe what happened on the night of June 21?

A. The surprising thing was that the house had been pretty peaceful for two or three days. We watched a movie on TV, got the girls to bed, had some lemonade, and then went upstairs to go to bed.

Q. How did you first know something was wrong?

A. The way I came awake, I guess.

Q. There was something different about it?

A. Yes, it was like I'd been—oh, thrown off a cliff or something. You know, as if some violent action woke me up.

Q. Can you describe what you saw?

A. At first I didn't see anything at all. I just felt this tremendous sort of panic—I wasn't sure if I was having a nightmare or not.

Q. What convinced you that you weren't having a nightmare?

A. Her scales.

Q. [Pause.] Her scales. You mean by that serpentine—snakelike—scales?

A. Yes.

Q. You said "she." These scales were on a woman?

A. Yes.

Q. Would you describe her?

A. (Pause on tape.) To be honest, I even hate to think about her. (Pause again.) Her skin was paper white, but it was covered in some places with the scaly surface I mentioned, and then in other places with open sores, the kind you'd think a leper would have or something. And these sores were running with pus.

Q. How old was she?

A. I would estimate around sixty-five or seventy. I can't be sure.

Q. What else did you first notice about her?

A. She had long, white, scraggly hair and her eyes were all red and the inside of her mouth and her gums were green. Some of her teeth were missing but those she had were very long and vampirelike.

Q. What about her body?

A. That was the weird thing. Her body itself was firm, you know, like that of a younger woman.

Q. What did she do?

A. [Long pause.] She paralyzed me in some way. I saw her walking out of the shadows to our bed and I sensed what she was going to do but I couldn't stop her.

Q. Then what?

A. Then she mounted me in the dominant position and she started riding me. That's the only way I can describe it.

Q. Was it pleasurable?

A. No, no. In fact, I don't remember feeling anything at all, other than panic and complete terror.

Q. What was Janet doing during all this?

A. Only after I'd been awake for a time did I realize that Janet had earlier gone downstairs to sleep on the couch, which she occasionally does in the hot months.

Q. What about the succubus? What was it doing?

A. Coming to a sexual climax. She just looked at me and smiled showing those incredible teeth. I tried to look away but something held my eyes to her. I could tell when she was having orgasms because she would give little jerks and her smile would broaden.

Q. She was having orgasms?

A. Oh, yes, you could tell that by her expressions and her movements.

Q. Then what happened?

A. Then she vanished.

Q. Just like that?

A. Just like that. Just vanished. And that's when I noticed the sticky substance all over me.

Q. Sticky substance?

A. Yes. I suppose you'd have to compare it to semen, the texture of it, anyway. It was emitted from the creature's vagina. And I was sore, too.

Q. Sore?

A. Yes, as if I'd had prolonged sex, even though it had been only a few minutes. But then I began to wonder if I hadn't passed out during it or something because, as I said, my genitals were extremely sore.

Q. Did you have any idea what had happened?

A. I called Ed Warren in the morning and he told me all about succubi, that they don't have any gender, but that a devil that rapes a man is known as a succubus, and one that rapes a woman is known as an incubus.

Q. What happened next?

A. I went into the bathroom and looked myself over. The fluid on my body had a very pungent odor. I took a shower and washed it off as quickly as I could. I had to scrub very hard. Then I went downstairs to tell Janet what had happened.

Q. What was her reaction?

A. She started crying and said that no matter what, she was going to see that the church got involved in our problem and help resolve it. She said that the very first thing she was going to do in the morning was call the diocese office. [Pause.] Then something even odder happened.

Q. What was that?

A. The next morning, at breakfast, my daughter Dawn talked about a dream she'd had about me being attacked by this horrible, ugly woman. [Pause.] She saw this hag with teeth missing and sores all over her body having sex with me. The thing was,

I hadn't told the kids about the attack. Dawn couldn't possibly have known about my rape except through her nightmare. Both Janet and I were really startled and upset by this. It just seemed to make Janet calling the diocese office all the more important.

Q. So she called?

A. Yes. Next day.

Q. Did they cooperate?

A. No—it turned out to be almost as terrifying as the succubus itself.

Promising
Phone Call

*T*he Roman Catholic Church is a bureaucracy in every sense of the word. Power is delegated in varying levels from the Vatican to literally every corner of the world.

Following the attack of the succubus, which proved to both the Smurls and the Warrens that the demon was increasing the severity of its attack, Janet Smurl resolved to get the church directly involved in the haunting, no matter what it took.

Janet: "I suppose I was a little angry when I called that morning. Here I'd been a faithful Catholic all my life but my church wasn't helping at all." She smiles. "I'm slow to anger but once I get worked up, I can be pretty formidable."

Janet was prepared to make her case argumentatively if need be.

Jack at work, the children at school, she sat down next to the phone, looked up the number of the diocese office, and called.

The receptionist put Janet on hold and a few minutes later a man who identified himself as Father O'Leary picked up the phone.

"Good morning," the priest said. He sounded robust and intelligent and friendly.

"Hello, father. My name is Janet Smurl. I'm a parishioner in West Pittston."

"That's a nice town."

"Yes, it is, father." She drew herself up and said, "Father, I need to talk to you about some problems we've been having here."

"Family problems?"

"Not exactly, father. It's about a haunting."

There was a brief silence on the other end. "A haunting. I see."

"I'm not a hysterical woman, father."

"I'm sure you're not, Janet. Why don't you tell me about it?"

"Then you believe in hauntings, father?"

"Of course I do."

Janet could scarcely believe what she was hearing. She'd been prepared for battle. This priest was not only not arguing or evading, he was agreeing with her.

"It's been terrible," Janet said, letting some of her feelings come through clearly in her voice.

"Why don't you tell me about it, dear?"

So Janet told him. Everything. From the first rappings in the wall to the rocking chair that creaked by itself, as if somebody invisible were sitting in it—to the rape last night.

"This is very serious," Father O'Leary said. "Very serious."

"And the problem is, we can't get anybody in the church to help us. Not in any serious way, anyway."

"What if I go to the chancellor?"

"Do you mean it?"

"Yes," Father O'Leary said, "I do mean it. And I'll be happy to make your case for you. I think that once all the facts are laid out, the chancellor will get very interested in this case."

"It's almost too much to hope for," Janet said, feeling hope for the first time in many long and dark months.

"Why don't you let me do some talking to the chancellor and then you can give me a call tomorrow morning. How would that be?"

"That would be great, father." Tears filled Janet's eyes. "I can't thank you enough, father." Gently, the priest said, "Just call me tomorrow, dear."

When Jack got home that evening, Janet rushed to tell him the news about Father O'Leary and how helpful he was.

Soon Jack himself was on the phone, calling a friend who knew several people in the diocese office. The friend had been skeptical about church officials helping them out. When Jack told the man about Father O'Leary, the friend said, "I've never heard of a Father O'Leary there."

"Well, Janet talked to him," Jack said, defensively.

"You sure his name was O'Leary?"

"Positive."

"Tell you what, Jack. Why don't you let me do a little checking and get back to you."

Jack laughed sourly. "We're finally getting a little cooperation and you want to spoil it."

"I just want to be sure everything is on the up and up."

"All right," Jack said, "get back to me then."

Twenty minutes later the phone rang. It was Jack's friend.

"I called a priest who's a buddy of mine and who knows everybody in the diocese office."

"And?"

"And there's no Father O'Leary." He sighed. "I'm sorry, Jack."

"But Janet talked to him."

"I'm sorry, Jack. But listen, I do have a name for you at the diocese office. Father Gerald F. Mullally. He's chancellor of the Scranton office. He's a very decent guy, Jack. He really is."

So it was that the next day Janet Smurl again called the diocese office. This time she asked for Father Gerald Mullally.

He listened politely as Janet told him, first, about speaking with a Father O'Leary yesterday, and then about the haunting they'd been experiencing.

"Father O'Leary, you say?"

"Yes, father."

"I wish I could say there was a Father O'Leary here but I'm afraid there isn't."

So Jack's friend had been right, after all, a possibility that Janet had been trying to deny since last night.

"Do you know much about hauntings, father?"

As other priests had when she'd mentioned the supernatural, the cleric's voice became tight and guarded. "I am familiar with the phenomenon, yes."

Just then Janet realized that the demon could well be working overtime. Could it possibly have spoken to Janet on the telephone in the voice of a Father O'Leary, thereby not only making a fool out of her and instilling her with false hope, but also damaging her credibility with this priest, the chancellor?

"It really happened, father. I really did talk to a Father O'Leary." She realized how plaintive her voice sounded and was embarrassed for herself.

"Why don't I take this matter under consideration, Mrs. Smurl, and get back to you tomorrow. How would that be?"

"That would be fine. I'd really appreciate it."

That evening the spirits were quiet. The Smurls had a relaxed dinner of pork chops, fried potatoes, and salad. They were in good moods because of the prospect of the church finally intervening. Janet's talk with the chancellor himself had considerably helped the entire family's state of mind.

Next day Janet spent all day by the telephone.

She was so afraid of missing the call that she did not do her vacuuming, fearful the sound would drown out the phone. When she went to the bathroom, she left the door open. Even doing

122

dishes, she ran the water slowly so that the sound wouldn't turn into a roar.

Each time the phone rang, she dove for it, only to be disappointed by the identity of the caller.

It was never the diocese.

As soon as Jack came through the door, he said, "Hi, honey." He kissed her on the cheek and then he noticed the sadness in her eyes. "What's wrong?"

"He didn't call."

"What?"

"He didn't call."

"But he promised."

Janet just shook her head. "Some promise."

In bed that night, Janet, still depressed, said, "The church is never going to help us, are they?"

"I wish I could say yes but I'm afraid the answer is no."

Unfortunately, Jack's word was to prove true.

The official church would never be of any real help, even though they did eventually dispatch a priest to satisfy the outcry of the Smurls' Catholic friends.

Chris Makes a Discovery

At six feet, 260 pounds, Chris McKinnell is a man with an easy laugh that is quite often aimed at himself and his liking for rich foods.

As a professional demonologist, Chris quickly became a close friend of the Smurls because he was both good company and a great help in explaining all the terrible sounds and sights that had been filling the family home.

The week that Janet talked to "Father O'Leary," Chris spent many hours at the Smurl house and his diary notes the following phenomena:

◆ Heavy rappings at John's and Mary's house and the sound of animal hooves—almost "a clippety-clop" sound, running across the walls and ceiling of the duplex
◆ Holding a crucifix up to the strange rapping sounds in the wall and thereby driving the demon out

♦ Scratchings from Mary's side of the hutch that sounded like rats in the walls

♦ A drop in temperature that nearly froze Janet and Chris as they tried to "clear" one of the bedrooms of demons

♦ An incredible stench that came as Chris started chanting to fill a room with Christ's love, a stench that drove everybody down the stairs

♦ Janet being immobilized by some invisible force ("I can't move," she said to Chris when he asked her to cross the room. "It feels like rushing water is holding me back.")

♦ Vapor issuing from Chris's mouth as if he were standing in subzero temperatures, even though the room in which Chris and Jack stood was measured at approximately seventy degrees

"The infestation has really gotten bad over here," Chris reported to the Warrens on the phone. "I don't know how much more they can take. There was even evidence of an incubus."

He then related to them an incident in which the sleeping Janet had been sexually assaulted but not raped. He also played for them a most disturbing tape. After recording the ominous sounds of the wall-rappings, Chris had picked up something he hadn't counted on. As the tape unspooled, you could hear the sounds of pigs squealing.

Lorraine and Ed, listening on extension phones on the other end, both realized that in the most serious infestations, the oinking of pigs is a familiar sound, pigs always being symbolic of a harsh demonic presence.

"We have to do something," Chris said.

Grimly, Ed replied, "Yes, we do, Chris. And fast."

The First Exorcism

*O*f all the Roman Catholic Church's rituals, none is more complex than an exorcism. The priest performing the ceremony must make certain beforehand that all family members are in the state of grace and are willing to truly give themselves over to the healing blood of Christ.

In the experience of the Warrens, some exorcisms don't work because the families involved have not honestly declared themselves clean in spirit, and in other cases the demonic forces are so strong that they simply cannot be overcome.

The priest the Warrens called on to help with the ritual was Father Robert F. McKenna of Monroe, Connecticut. He was a traditionalist, which means that he broke with the church after the Second Vatican Council twenty-five years ago, when Rome insisted that the mass be said in English and that other fundamental changes in faith be altered, too. Father McKenna found that many lay Catholics agreed with him. His parish was filled every Sunday morning with the faithful who chose to follow the old ways.

The exorcism, as the Warrens warned the Smurls, proved to enrage the demon, who knew what was about to happen.

The night before the ceremony, Jack found two strange, glowing women, one seemingly about forty, the other about twenty, wearing bonnets and long dresses, standing at the foot of his bed. They were, of course, the same two women who had visited him months earlier.

This time, however, they were accompanied by a man with light blond hair and the creases of middle age on his face.

When Jack tried to sit up and shout them out of the bedroom, he found that the entities had paralyzed him.

Jack: "I was totally immobilized as they stood there and talked among themselves. Then the man leaned forward and shook his finger at me. 'You'll pay for this!' he said. It was obvious he was very angry."

The three visitors remained in the bedroom another five minutes, whispering, pointing even, and at one moment, laughing at him.

Then the man of the trio looked angry again, his face twisted into an expression of absolute rage. "As I said, you'll pay for this," he repeated, and then they were gone as suddenly as they'd appeared.

After a few minutes, feeling and movement returned to Jack's limbs. He woke Janet and told her what had happened. They spent the rest of the night huddled in each other's arms.

While the research team went separately to the Smurls', Ed and Lorraine drove their van toward the New York State line.

But suddenly Ed, who was driving, was seized by cramps and a high degree of fever. His vision became blurred and he became so weak that he had to pull over on the macadam.

"What's wrong, honey?" Lorraine asked, obviously concerned.

"Some kind of bug. You know how the flu can come on."

Yes, Lorraine thought. Flu or—other things.

They sat on the roadside watching cars hurtle by in the brilliant daylight. Ed only seemed weaker.

Finally, Lorraine said, "Dear, I think we'd better turn back."

"I hate to do that," Ed said. But his voice reflected his condition. He was barely audible.

Lorraine got out of the van, walked around to the driver's side, and took the wheel.

She knew that there was only one place for Ed at this point—bed.

She found the exit ramp and headed back home.

In the hours before the ceremony, the Smurls went around their house opening the doors to cupboards, closets, and anywhere else that spirits might hide while the sacred rite was taking place.

Throughout the morning, the Smurls had been speculating what the ceremony would be like. Movies and television like to exaggerate such things. For this reason, Janet and Jack were apprehensive about what would actually take place.

When they visited with John and Mary on the other side of the duplex, they found that the older couple shared their anxiety. They comforted each other by recalling all the reassuring things the Warrens had said about Father McKenna.

Janet went back to her side of the house first and when she reached the kitchen, she found the room filled with the scent of roses. Quickly she called Jack and Dawn in from the front porch. They smelled the rich, sweet scent of the roses, too. Janet felt an optimism she hadn't known in more than a year. Even the prospect of the exorcism was filling the house with God's love and driving out the demon.

At two o'clock that afternoon, the fifty-nine-year-old Father McKenna pulled up in front of the Smurl duplex and parked his car. He is a man with light brown hair, eyeglasses, and a gentle voice; his large, powerful hands reflect his inner strength. He had grown up working hard and those years of sheer grit had helped him through the physically draining performance of more than fifty exorcisms, twenty of which had been successful.

The priest introduced himself to all those gathered in the living room—Jack, Janet, Dawn, Heather, Shannon, Carin, John and Mary Smurl, and Mike from the Warren team.

The Smurls had turned a table into an altar. The priest had told them how, after combining the rites of exorcism with the saying of mass in traditional Latin style, the demon would, it was hoped, flee.

"We need to pray harder than we ever have in our lifetimes," Father McKenna said as he opened the black leather doctor's bag in which he kept the altar candles, cruets for water and wine, a missal and missal stand, small hand bells, and a gold chalice. As the priest set up the various articles he needed to say mass, the room took on the appearance of a small chapel with nine parishioners gathered for a special ritual.

Once again, the priest said, "I ask you to pray for the salvation of your souls and to drive the demons out. I'd also ask you not to offer me anything of monetary value because that could hamper the exorcism."

Then he went upstairs to Dawn's and Heather's bedroom and put on his vestments. When he came back downstairs, he wore a white wool habit of the Dominican order, and the ankle-length tunic of the vestment. A purple silk stole was around his neck and shoulders, and around his waist was a large fifteen-decade rosary, with the beads hanging on the left side of his body off a belt.

The exorcism was about to begin, one of the truly ancient rituals of the Roman Catholic Church. The purple stole the priest wears around his neck symbolizes penance and thus humility, the priest begging God through prayers to free the infested home or person. Similarly, part of the ritual consists of adjurations to the devil, demanding that Satan, in the name of Christ, the Blessed Virgin and all the saints, leave the person or home immediately. In some cases, the ritual consists of the priest demanding that the spirit or spirits who have caused the infestation speak out and identify themselves. (Bishop McKenna, for example, has talked with many demons in the course of performing his exorcisms.) Finally, there are the instruments the priest uses: holy water, a crucifix, and a relic of a saint, which is applied to the body in the same fashion—touched to the head or breast, for example—in the course of the exorcism. Despite the portrayals seen in recent movies, there is no chanting or singing at exorcisms. The priest prays in a loud, strong voice and, in the instance of Bishop McKenna, does so in Latin. *Dominus vobiscum* (the Lord be with you). The ritual begins.

"Now," Father McKenna said, "I'll go into every room on both sides of the duplex and recite the prayers of exorcism. Then I'll sprinkle the rooms with holy water." He explained that he'd like Janet and Jack to accompany him on his rounds and that he would also exorcise the basement, the attic, the long backyard, and the small front yard.

The first stop was Janet and Jack's bedroom.

"Ecce crucem Domini, fugite partes adversae," the priest said in Latin. In English this meant, "Behold the cross of the Lord, flee adverse enemies."

As they listened to the long address the priest made to God and Satan alike—"Seize the dragon, the ancient serpent who is the devil and Satan, and cast him bound into the abyss that he may no more seduce the nations"—Jack and Janet feared that the demon might choose this time to set the room afire or something equally drastic.

But there was no sign of the demon as they went room to room, and finally they were back downstairs where Jack, who had been an altar boy, assisted Father McKenna in saying a traditional Latin mass.

Then their fears were confirmed.

As Janet and Jack knelt at the makeshift altar, they heard, coming from upstairs, the sounds of a child throwing a tantrum. A very young child. One who did not belong in the Smurl household. Then from the kitchen they heard cupboard doors beginning to bang shut. In front of them, just beyond Father McKenna, knickknacks and plants began to vibrate.

Father McKenna only said the mass prayers all the louder, as if to spite Satan. Janet and Jack squeezed hands together and prayed as they never had before.

The child's rage upstairs grew louder.

The priest raised the chalice, celebrating the Son of Man and the Son of God.

And then finally the aberrations ceased.

The child's irate voice could be heard no longer. The house ceased its trembling. And the scent of roses could once more be smelled.

For now, anyway, the power of prayer seemed to be more powerful than the power of darkness.

After he had completed the mass, Father McKenna asked the Smurls to fill up a bucket of water. He blessed the water and told them to sprinkle it if any supernatural disturbances broke out after he left.

In preparation for the exorcism, Father Mckenna had been on a partial fast for three days, eating just one full meal daily. Janet offered to make him dinner, but the priest had only a cup of hot chocolate and a piece of cake.

The Smurls told the priest how much they appreciated what he'd done for them.

In return, Father McKenna stressed the fact that they should not give the demon "recognition." "That's the worst thing you can do," he told them.

"But it's hard not to talk about it," Jack said. "For all of us."

"That's where you must help each other," the friendly priest explained. "Be sure not to mention it and I think things will be better for you."

Then Father McKenna gave their house a general blessing and said, "I should start back now."

Janet came up and took his arm "We can't thank you enough, father."

The scent of roses drifted in from the kitchen. The girls smiled and said good-bye to the priest. There was the feeling that they had passed some kind of test today, that the Devil had pushed them to the breaking point but they had not broken. As a family, they had remained holy and moral and intact.

"Good-bye," the priest said.

They walked him to the car, Janet still making offers of various foods she could pack for him.

The priest smiled and said no. "Denying yourself is good for both body and soul."

He started the car and waved to them and was gone.

The Smurls went back inside. There was a definite feeling of elation throughout both sides of the duplex.

Could the demon be banished?

One way or the other, the coming days would give them a clear signal.

ED WARREN:

Lorraine and I stayed in constant touch with the Smurls in the hours and days following the exorcism. I only gradually overcame the mysterious illness that forced us back from Father McKenna's service and even three days later was having trouble holding food down and walking (a buzzing sound having filled my head).

Unfortunately, the word from the Smurls was not good, attesting to just how powerful the demon we were dealing with really was.

Into our Smurls' file went the following items:

◆ Tapping and hissing noises were reported by Mary Smurl on her side of the duplex.

◆ The smell of raw sewage overwhelmed Mary Smurl as she was doing housework one day.

◆ Clothing began disappearing from Dawn's room, causing an argument between her and Heather. Finally they realized that the demon was once again "hiding" things to cause trouble between family members.

◆ Dawn watched as earrings lifted themselves from her jewelry box and began flying past her eyes.

◆ The family became so intimidated by a feeling of the demon in the house that they began going out to the garage to talk about it lest they grant it recognition.

In the midst of all this, the Smurls had to deal with yet another problem.

One night Janet called us and said, in tears, "Little Carin has been so sick that she's lost seven pounds in less than thirty-six hours. All Jack and I can think about is the man who appeared and said 'You'll pay for this!' It's the demon getting back at us, isn't it?"

I tried to remain as calm, and calming, as I could but the news over the next few days was the sort that can devastate parents.

Carin Smurl got so sick that she had to be hospitalized for a week. The doctors did everything they could but at first nothing seemed to help lower her fever or stop her from losing weight.

Finally, Janet called one night and said, "Thank God, Ed, her fever broke today." At last the doctors took control of the little girl's life.

But by now we knew sadly and for certain, as did Father McKenna, that the exorcism had failed.

We had no idea if Carin's illness had been caused by the infestation, but even if it hadn't been, all the other signs pointed to a demon sure of itself and still very much a presence in the Smurl home.

THE APPRENTICE DEMONOLOGIST:

David Wilson: "Two days after I read about Ed and Lorraine Warren, I contacted them at their office and told them how interested I'd become in the field of the paranormal. Unlike the others I'd met, I found them to be very human and—well, 'normal,' I guess you'd say. The thing I liked about them right away was that while they took what they did very seriously, they also laughed a lot. They had a real perspective on their work and that put me at ease right away. I wanted to know everything about them and their work I could, so they suggested that I start out by attending one of their lectures. 'Demonology interests a lot of people,' Lorraine told me, 'but very few stay with it. I think you'll see why once you've been at one of our lectures.' "

A week and a half later, David Wilson drove his parents' Dodge to a small upstate college where he found an auditorium packed with people of all ages, not just the students he'd expected.

Because of the subzero temperature outside, the windows were covered with frost that the moonlight turned into silver as the lights went down and the Warrens began the first part of their lecture, a slide show.

David Wilson: "I'd never seen or heard anything like it. Here was physical evidence, slide by slide, that the paranormal worlds we hear about actually exist, delivered in a calm, rational manner. There were slides of ghosts and slides of psychic lights and slides of objects being levitated and materialized. Ed told of seeing a four-hundred-pound refrigerator being raised from the floor by invisible forces, of a console television set being lifted and then hurled to the floor, and of becoming involved with the Lutzes, the family whose plight became known as The Amityville Horror.

"After the Warrens concluded the slide show, they took questions from the audience. I'd never dreamed that so many people had had paranormal experiences, but here were all these people—some very well educated and well dressed, some poor and not especially well-spoken—sharing experiences in an almost support-group kind of setting. The evening could not have been long enough for me. Unfortunately because a blizzard was brewing outside, everything had to be cut short after two hours. Afterward, as the Warrens were getting bundled up for their trip home, I went up to them and said that I was interested in becoming a demonologist. Lorraine and Ed looked very happy about this, but Lorraine warned me again, 'Not everybody stays with the program, David.' 'Why?' I asked. She looked at Ed and said, 'Fear. Just that simple. There's a lot of stress involved, as you'll find.' But I really wasn't paying attention. All I'd wanted to hear was that they were going to accept me as one of their students. 'So I can come up to your office?' I asked. Ed put out his hand, laughed, and clapped me on the back. He said, 'Welcome aboard, David.' "

They scheduled a meeting for a week later, when others would gather at the Warren home, and once again David found himself counting minutes, hours, days till the time finally rolled around.

Demon in the Shower

*F*ollowing the exorcism, the Smurls were naturally optimistic about their future. The scent of roses lingered, the walls were quiet.

For a few hours at least.

During this time the phone scarcely stopped ringing. By this time there were many in West Pittston who were well aware of what was happening to the Smurls. They called, as concerned friends, to see how the family was doing following the religious rites.

Those who called six days following the exorcism heard about Carin's illness. Those who called a few days later were even more shocked.

Sixteen-year-old Dawn was in the bathroom. She had taken her clothes off in preparation for a shower. She would recall later hearing a rapping in the wall but assumed it was nothing more than the usual—the demon reminding the family of its constant presence.

Dawn ran water, testing it so it would be just the right temperature, then climbed into the shower. She soaped herself and leaned her head back against the wall, letting the water splash over her face. She felt relaxed after a long day at school.

Then she felt something seize her arms.

In front of her now she sensed a presence, an invisible entity that brushed against her the way a man would. Its intent was clear.

For the moment, however, it contented itself with squeezing her arms until her eyes ran with painful tears.

She pushed away from the entity then and hurled herself out through the plastic shower curtain. Instantly she began screaming for her parents.

She grabbed a towel that was on the rack and ran from the bathroom, still shouting to her parents for help.

After they had calmed their daughter, Janet and Jack began asking their daughter questions.

They had no doubt about what had happened. If the incubus had materialized, it would have raped their own sixteen-year-old daughter in their own home.

Lorraine Warren:

Ed kept in constant contact with the Smurls following Dawn's near rape. Several team members took turns making the trip to West Pittston.

What they reported was not encouraging.

♦ The demon continued to roam back and forth between duplexes, inflicting on John Smurl a body temperature drop so severe that not even several blankets could stop him from shivering, his teeth literally clattering despite the best efforts of his wife Mary to warm him.

 ♦ Janet woke up one morning with gouge marks on her right arm. The marks were almost two inches long. One of her fingers was swollen and had a deep puncture mark in it, as if she had been bitten by something.

 ♦ Mary Smurl also found slash marks on her arms.

 ♦ One day before she went shopping, Janet put the family dog, Simon, in the yard, which is enclosed by a chain-link fence. Janet locked all the doors in the house. There was no way the dog could have gotten back inside, yet when she returned home she found Simon in the living room.

 ♦ An incubus began to take shape in the bathtub as Janet bathed one evening, a creature no more than three feet tall with a gelantinous coating covering its gnarled body. Before it could completely materialize, Janet jumped from the tub, wrapped a towel around herself, and ran down the hall to her bedroom.

 ♦ Mary Smurl told Janet that water faucets in the house had been turning off and on by themselves and pots and pans were disappearing. She had also found a stench in her bedroom so bad that she could not enter the room. Janet got the holy water Father McKenna had given her and said to the demon, "I command you to be gone." Almost immediately they could feel the demonic smell leaving this room and entering the next one. They went from room to room, praying and sprinkling holy water. Finally, the smell was gone.

 ♦ On her way back from the supermarket one day, Janet noticed the smell of rotten garbage filling the family car. She pulled over to the roadside, took out the holy water she kept with her constantly, and drove the smell away.

 ♦ Apparitions began to plague the Smurls again. One day, for example, Jack was watching television when he saw a young man, about twenty-five years old, with long blond hair and an unpleasant smile, watching him from across the room. When Jack started to get out of his chair, the young man vanished.

◆ Jack was once again levitated from his bed and then hurled brutally to the floor.

◆ A visiting relative was driving past the Smurl duplex when he saw an elderly woman with very long white hair standing in the window, staring out at him. The woman began to levitate and float back and forth before the startled man's eyes.

◆ Mary Smurl once again saw the faceless black form and this time she became so depressed that none of the Smurl family could comfort her. In poor health, she alternated between long periods of silence and withdrawal and intense jags of sobbing.

Over the phone one night, Ed and I explained again to the Smurls that there were four demonic stages, and that these were infestation, oppression, possession, and death. Under infestation, the demon and spirits enter a house; this is followed by oppression, when the family comes under attack and harassment. In the possession stage, a demon can move into and possess a human being's body. Death was the ultimate goal of this demon, of that we had no doubt. I don't think the Smurls did either.

Which was why we suggested they spend a long weekend at their favorite campground.

"You know," Jack said, "that sounds like a great idea. Just pack up the family and take off."

"Exactly," I said. "It will help you get your mind off things."

If only we could have known what awaited them.

Dark Outing

*S*ometime around noon on a Friday the Smurl family put their food, soda, coffee, cooler, and other camping utensils in their eight-passenger maroon and silver 1979 Chevrolet van. On the hood of the van a friend had lettered The Smurlmobile in white letters and maroon trim.

It was a hot day and the Smurls were in a good mood as they made their way past Scranton and drove northeast toward the campground near Honesdale. After they arrived and began unpacking, Jack became uneasy. The Smurls had been to this campground many times and always enjoyed themselves, but Jack Smurl felt something was wrong now.

"I don't understand it, but I have a feeling of evil," Jack said to Janet. Janet was surprised to hear this because of the good fun they always had in the outdoors. "What do you mean by something evil, Jack? How would you define it?" she asked.

Jack got a bit edgy. "I can't describe it in words except that

I just have bad feelings," he said. Along with being a hot day, it was also humid, and for a few minutes there was an air of tension between Jack and Janet. Neither one of them wanted to see the weekend ruined, and despite the problems in the house, getting away to the Poconos had always made them feel good.

They decided to concentrate on having a good time. Along with swimming, there was a playground for the children, a recreation room, and the open spaces of the forest. They put on the "pop-up," the plastic top that goes on the back of the camper. This provided welcome shade because there were only a few trees on the site.

The day passed normally and when Saturday dawned another hot day was on the way. In the afternoon, Janet and the children were out and Jack was sitting in the shade of the van with Simon.

Jack and Simon were facing the clothesline where Janet had tied five bathing suits on the line and draped half a dozen towels over the rope. There was no wind blowing, but suddenly all of the suits and towels fell off the line at the same time. Startled, Simon jumped up and looked toward the line. Jack was also taken by surprise, because he knew that Janet had tied the bathing suits securely. He was curious as to how everything had fallen off the line simultaneously, but he didn't dwell on it.

That night, Janet and the kids all went to the recreation hall to play bingo. At the time Dawn was sixteen, Heather was fourteen, the twins were nine, and their cousin Billy was fourteen. The youngsters got along well and they enjoyed doing things with Janet.

When it became dark Jack decided to build a fire. About 9:15 P.M. the wood crackled and the blaze got stronger. Simon was sitting by Jack when the dog again became startled, as he had that afternoon, except this time Simon growled and looked over toward some bushes.

Jack turned his head toward the bushes and to his astonishment there was a teenage girl standing there, about fourteen years old, with long, blond hair, almost to her waist, and dressed in a long, Colonial-style dress.

The girl was standing about thirty feet from Jack near the road and by the bushes. Jack saw her clearly; she was looking at him and smiling. Simon continued to growl, and Jack didn't understand this because Simon has a friendly disposition and likes youngsters.

Almost transfixed, Jack stared at the girl and she continued to smile back without moving. After about ten seconds, the girl vanished into thin air. A few seconds later she reappeared, then quickly disappeared again.

Jack thought that someone might be playing a trick on him. He went into the van and brought out a large flashlight with a four-inch-circumference beam. Jack looked over to the bushes and the girl was back again. She just stood there motionless, smiling at Jack. With Simon growling, Jack and the dog moved toward the girl. She disappeared.

Jack and Simon went to the spot where the girl had been standing but she was not to be found. Using the flashlight, Jack looked down the road and around the bushes but found nothing.

Later on, Janet and the children returned to the van. Shannon and Carin went to bed and sometime around midnight, Jack, Janet, Dawn, Heather, and Billy were sitting around the fire, drinking soda and snacking, when they heard a young girl's voice coming from across the lake.

The near shore of the lake was about 50 or 60 yards from where the Smurls were situated, and across the lake was another 150 yards. In the quiet of the night, they heard the voice call out, "Help me . . . help me."

Jack stayed with Heather and the twins. Billy, a strapping teenager who is a wrestler and football player, went with Janet and Dawn to the other side of the lake to determine if someone was in trouble. They took the flashlight with them, walked around the lake, and called out, but they didn't hear the voice again. Since no one had returned their call, they thought it might have been a prank.

On their way back to the van, they were walking past the small grocery store by the recreation hall when they were stopped dead in their tracks by what was taking place. Although there was no breeze, a heavy fifty-gallon metal trash can started to spin around furiously just a few feet from them. The floodlight from the store was on, and they could clearly see that the can was spinning very quickly. Jack, who was waiting for them to return, looked out and also saw the can spinning.

Janet, Dawn, and Billy looked at each other as the can continued to spin on its own for twenty or thirty seconds. The spinning then stopped abruptly and the can fell over. There was no animal inside and still no wind.

After hearing the girl's voice and now this, Janet, Dawn, and Billy were unnerved. "Let's get out of here," Dawn screamed, and the three of them rushed over to where Jack was waiting by the van.

They grouped around the fire, all of them frightened. Jack decided to tell them what had happened with the clothesline, and about the girl he had seen. The Smurls searched their minds for logical explanations but couldn't come up with any.

They left the campground the next day to drive home to West Pittston. Jack and Janet wondered if they were imagining all this?

The apparition of the young girl and the violently spinning garbage can proved one thing to Janet and Jack Smurl—that the Warrens were right. Ed and Lorraine had told them that the demon could travel with them.

The demon reinforced this on their way home. Halfway there, a terrible and unexplainable vibration began moving through the van, almost like huge sound waves that could crumble solid edifices in their wake. Jack had to pull over to the roadside before the vibrations stopped.

THE APPRENTICE DEMONOLOGIST:

A steep road led to a formidable house tucked into a deep cavern of shadows. The yellow light spilling from the windows seemed particularly inviting. David Wilson, still as excited as he had been a week earlier, pulled into the driveway behind several other cars and then went inside.

Two hours later he found himself one of seven people still spellbound by a presentation of charts, photographs, artifacts, and tape recordings, each of which revealed a special aspect of the spirit world.

Seated around him were a policeman, a dentist, a service station manager, a college student, a nun, and a certified public accountant.

First Ed and then Lorraine had talked, and then a man who revealed his first experience as an apprentice demonologist. David attributed the man's nervousness to simple anxiety over having to stand up in front of a group. But he soon realized that what the man was nervous about was his experience in accompanying Ed and Lorraine.

The man, tall, thin, wearing a blue turtleneck sweater and a tweed sport coat with sleeves not quite long enough to cover his wrists, stabbed the button of a tape recorder and said: "I went into a room by myself with a tape recorder and this is what I brought back."

At first all David could hear was ambient sound in the room—the machine itself running. But then a rapping started, slowly and faintly at first, then increasingly sharp and more frequent. Then the rapping was joined by an eerie panting sound, as if a huge animal had run out of breath. Then the rapping became gigantic thuds.

David watched the man's face pale as the tape rolled on. He also noticed that the man's left eye had developed a tic.

When the man was finished, Ed began giving an impromptu lecture about some of his experiences in demonology.

♦ *Seeing a crucifix literally explode when a demonic spirit focused on it*

♦ *Examining a human skull used for drinking blood during satanic ceremonies*

♦ *Studying a rag doll used by a demonic spirit that began to exert control over a very young girl*

♦ *Watching bottles of bleach and detergent being levitated behind him as he ascended basement steps*

♦ *Validating the authenticity of a psychic photograph taken in Mendon, Massachusetts that clearly shows the presence of a ghost*

Ed related many other incidents, then recommended that serious students of demonology study such books as Padre Pio: The Stigmatist *by Reverend Charles M. Carty;* True and False Possession *by Jean Lhermitte; and* Poltergeist over England *by Harry Price.*

At the end of the night's meeting, David saw the man who had spoken go up to Ed, say something softly, and then put out his hand. Ed shook it. Neither was smiling. The man then went over to the hall closet, got his coat, and left.

David sensed what had gone on but left it for Ed to confirm. Addressing the remaining six students, Ed said: "Harold has decided to drop out. I don't think I have to tell you that his encounter at the house we took him to shook him very deeply. He said that he's slept very little since that night, and that he's lost his appetite, and that his wife is against him going on in demonology. I think right now he needs our prayers, so why don't we take a few minutes right now and say a short rosary for him."

David, though not a Catholic, willingly joined in the prayers.

He had had his first glimpse of a man whose existence had been threatened by the supernatural. It was a glimpse he would never forget.

The Assault Continues

Q. Janet, would you describe some of the events that took place after you returned from camping out?

A. Well, the night we got home Shannon was levitated, and it took us several hours to calm her down. And then Mary.

Q. What about Mary?

A. To be honest, all of us had this fear in the back of our minds that the demon would do something that would cause her to have a heart attack.

Q. Something like that happened?

A. [Pause.] The black form came into Mary's bedroom and it frightened her so much that—

Q. That what?

A. That we were afraid—

Q. What else happened?

A. Shannon was thrown out of bed. Very violently. We heard the noise in the middle of the night and ran down the hall and found her on the floor, badly bruised and sobbing.

Q. Did she remember what happened?

A. She said that the dark form had appeared and thrown her out of bed, threw her so hard that she first hit the wall and then the floor. Then he spoke to her.

Q. What did he say?

A. "One strike, two strikes, three strikes and you're out." That was when Jack sort of went crazy. He saw Shannon there on the floor and he just couldn't take it anymore. He started shouting at the demon to show itself. He held a container of holy water in his hand and kept calling for the demon to come out. I was very proud of him. He wasn't afraid of the demon at all. He just wanted to have it out once and for all, even if it cost him his life. Then John and Mary came over.

Q. They'd heard the noise?

A. Yes, Shannon's being thrown out of bed had awakened everybody on our side. Then John and Mary heard that we were up so they came over to see if anything was wrong. John did something fantastic that night.

Q. What was that?

A. He brought over this certified relic he has, a wooden cross that contains a thread of the robe of Jesus Christ. He said, "I think the demon means to kill all of us. I didn't used to think that—I thought it just wanted to torment us—but now I think it wants our lives. So I want you and Jack to have this relic to protect yourselves with." "But if you don't have it, you won't have anything to protect yourself with," we said. Then Mary spoke up and said—and I'll never forget this—"We're old. If something happens to us, we've lived our lives. You have a family to raise. You take the relic." You could see the tears in Jack's eyes. He was really moved by this.

Q. Did things calm down?

A. Not really. For Jack, they even got worse at work. The demon wasn't satisfied with destroying our home lives, and even our lives at the campground where we'd been going for years. Now it even wanted to destroy Jack's job.

Testimony of Roberta Lupi

I have worked with Jack for many years at the company. I know him to be a reasonable, level-headed man not given to flights of fancy or wild imaginings.

I have to say, though, that when he first started telling me about some of the things going on around his house, I had some doubts. I thought there might be a natural explanation for these events.

Then the phone in our office started its really strange ringing.

One day, after Jack had explained to me how terrified he'd been the night before by being levitated, I was sitting at my desk when the phone started making this very strange noise, almost like a fire alarm going off, a very long, urgent burring. You almost had to cover your ears.

Over the next few months, this happened dozens of times. The phone company sent several repairmen but none of them could explain the eerie and irritating sounds coming from the phone.

Then one day the phone was accompanied by a very filthy odor, as if our office was a dank cellar, that kind of smell. We tried opening windows and spraying the area where we worked but that didn't help.

The smell was what convinced me that there really were supernatural forces working on Jack—the smell and the radio.

One day Jack, who looked more and more drained and exhausted from what was going on at home, asked me to listen to the radio on his desk. "Am I losing my mind, Roberta, or can you hear tappings inside the radio?"

I listened carefully. At first I didn't hear anything. But then I began to hear taps—one, two, three taps, like somebody was knocking on the radio with his knuckles. The intermittent tapping went on for several minutes and then it stopped.

"I'm sorry for you, Jack. I really am."

At church I asked the people in the congregation to start praying for the Smurls. I shared with the others the experiences I'd had with Jack and spoke of the supernatural forces that were working on him and his family.

None of us could imagine what such a strain would put on your health and sanity. Just from my brush with it—I'll never forget the sound the phone made or the stench in the office—I have to wonder how long I'd hold up under such an attack.

I don't know how the Smurls held on as long as they did.

While the Smurls were posing for this picture on May 19, 1987, eerie fluttering sounds were heard behind Janet and Jack. Sitting on the floor are twins Carin, left, and Shannon, who flank the family's German shepherd Simon. Kneeling behind the twins are Heather, left, and Dawn. Janet and Jack sit on a couch behind their children in the living room of the haunted house.

Top, Janet by the front door of the family's house. A creature disguised as a woman with ultra-white skin was outside the door one day, staring in at Janet.

Bottom, Janet and Jack in their bedroom.

Dawn explains to the author, Robert Curran, how the entity moved toward her while she was taking a shower.

Janet, left, Heather, in center, and Shannon re-create the day of Heather's confirmation when the light fixture came crashing down.

In the basement, Jack points to the wall where psychics say an earth-bound spirit named Abigail was standing.

Janet indicates how high she was levitated.

The twins in their bedroom. Shannon is on the top bunk and Carin sits on the bottom.

A view of Jack and Janet's living room, showing the staircase at left and the doorway to the kitchen at right.

Dawn, left, and her sister Heather show how they tape-recorded unexplained poundings that came from the inside of their closet.

Jack and Janet in front of their haunted house. They live on the left side of the duplex and Jack's parents reside on the right side.

From the side lawn, Jack and Janet look up at the second story of their house where neighbors heard unearthly screams and fluttering sounds when the Smurls were out of town.

The Smurl family gathers in the backyard. In the front row are twins Shannon, left, and Carin. Behind them, from left to right are Dawn, Jack, Janet, and Heather. Simon, the Smurls' German shepherd, stands near the rear porch of the house.

Janet opens the door of the family's van. The vehicle was violently pummeled by a steel-like invisible fist.

Top, John and Mary Smurl in their living room. In this room the temperature often dropped to a freezing cold, rapping noises came from furniture, and a strange animal ran across the floor.

Bottom, Ed and Lorraine Warren arrive at the Smurl residence and respond to questions from reporters.

Father Robert F. McKenna (who is now a bishop) performed three exorcisms in the Smurl house.

The hallway leading to Jack and Janet's bedroom. A mammoth, half-human, half-animal monster raced down this hallway at a horrified Jack Smurl.

Eerie Intrusion

*R*ain threatened in the dark gray afternoon. It was one of those days when the temperature was inexplicably more like October than July.

The girls were off playing, though the serious way that Dawn and Heather went at softball, Janet wondered if "playing" was the right word, and Jack was at work.

Janet had made a cabbage salad for dinner and put it in the refrigerator so it would be cold at dinner time.

The TV was on, a soap opera playing out its grim view of the human condition, when Janet began feeling a sudden headache and decided to lie down on the couch.

As she stretched out, she did not have to wonder why she had been having so many headaches lately. Ever since the camping experience, she and Jack had lived with the knowledge that even if they did sell the duplex and move, the demon might well move with them. So what was the point of going anywhere? If it could follow them to the camp, it could obviously follow them any-where.

She had been asleep approximately twenty minutes when she felt a very gentle touch, like fingers meant to arouse her sexually, begin to move up her thighs and then over her stomach and on up the rest of her body. Abruptly, she came fully awake.

Her first reaction was sarcasm: Here we go again. As ominous as the demon could be, it also reminded Janet, sometimes, of a small, irritating child bent on bothering its parent.

Janet waited a moment, then put her head back on the arm of the couch, intending to return to sleep. The headache was still pounding away.

She had not quite reached the point of sleep when she felt the touch return. She started up on the couch because this time the demon's touch was even more suggestive, moving carefully toward her belly.

But then what had seemed sexually abusive became something even more threatening—the demon's invisible hands found her throat and began choking her.

Janet could feel blood filling her face as she clawed out at her unseen assailant.

"Help!" She did her best to be heard but she knew there were two things against her. The demon's clutches were so tight she could barely get out a sound. And the house was empty. She couldn't yell loudly enough for Mary to hear.

She was thrown off the couch, the demon keeping the pressure on her. Janet saw the blackness of death come rushing at her and realized that her mind was beginning to give in to the blackness, the way drowning victims are said to surrender finally to their own overwhelming darkness.

Then she recalled what Ed Warren told her about imagining herself in the protective light of Christ's love. As she started to picture Christ in her mind, Simon came in from the kitchen where he'd been asleep, and seemed to sense what was going on in the room. The German shepherd crouched low, baring teeth dripping with saliva, ready to attack Janet's torturer.

Simon leapt through the air, snapping his jaws and reaching out with powerful paws, raking at the empty air. He landed next to the couch, still growling but frustrated now because he could not save the mistress he loved.

As for Janet, the picture of Christ she had conjured up became more and more vivid.

She saw the Savior with his hands reaching out to her. He wore flowing white robes and was bathed in a beautiful pearl-colored glow. In her mind, Janet reached out and accepted Christ's offer of help. As she moved toward him, she felt herself move within the protection of his beautiful spiritual light. Suddenly, she had a mental image of herself glowing in the same light in which Christ stood.

All the time this imaging process was going on, the demon's hands continued to strangle her, and she writhed and fought under the massive strength working on her throat. But the deeper she was drawn into the light surrounding Christ, the less effect the hands had on her breathing.

Simon continued to growl, trying to understand how he could help.

"Jesus, please protect me!"

The hands had loosened to the point that she could hear herself shout out now.

Once again, she cried, "Jesus, please protect me!"

By now the mental impression she had of being one with Jesus was nearly complete.

And so the demon's hands loosened even more until she could struggle to an upright position and grab a container of holy water nearby. She sprinkled drops of the pure water through the air.

And at last felt her throat free once more.

She had expected her first reaction to freedom—if, in fact, she did not die—to be one of relief.

But instead she sat on the edge of the couch sobbing almost without control. She had never been so close to death before and the sense of it had been terrifying. Only Christ and his light of love had saved her.

That night when she told Jack about the strangulation, he took her in his arms and held her for a very long time. Then he gathered the four children around them and together they thanked God for sparing Janet's life.

"I don't know what to do next," Janet said.

"I do," Jack said.

He went to the phone and called Ed Warren.

Speculation

*A*s he always did for exorcisms, Father McKenna fasted for his trip to the Smurls' in West Pittston, where he hoped to put an end once and for all to the curse that lay over the duplex like the most terrible lingering illness.

On the day of the second exorcism, the weather offered the cleric some pleasant views of rolling, verdant hills and cloudless blue sky.

He arrived near noon to find the Smurls and their children, and Mary and John as well, standing in the living room waiting for him.

Before he began the rite of exorcism, he talked a while with Janet and Jack, asking them to tell him about some of the things that had taken place since the first exorcism.

Watching them, listening to them, Father McKenna could assess just how strong the demon had become. He saw before him two people ravaged by a force they did not understand.

＊　＊　＊

Because he did not say mass this time, the ceremony was briefer. Father McKenna walked through every room on both sides of the duplex, dispensing holy water and ancient prayers in Latin. Then he blessed each member of the family individually. He even said a special animal blessing for Simon, all these prayers coming from the *Rituale Romanum,* a document of scarcely more than twenty-five pages that contains all the ancient prayers and incantations for dealing with demons. *"Dominus vobiscum,"* he said in the mass Latin of the traditional church.

When the priest had concluded his duties, Janet said, "There's one big difference between this time and last time."

"What's that?" Father McKenna asked.

"The demon hasn't done anything."

And so it hadn't.

During the first exorcism, the demon had rattled cupboards, taken the form of an angry youngster, and set foul odors on the air.

"Is that a good sign?" Janet asked.

Father McKenna said, "Let's hope so."

Janet and Jack once again asked the priest to stay for dinner but he said that he wished to continue his fast and, anyway, had several things to do back at the parish.

His eyes scanned the living room. He was long accustomed to the subtlest presence of demons, and he watched for such a sign now. Nothing. His ears were equally accustomed to the sounds of demons. He listened, and heard nothing.

Father McKenna bowed his head and said a silent prayer that the Smurls would now be left alone once and for all.

The Smurls bid the priest good-bye and walked him out to his car. Several neighbors, knowing the rite was going to take place that afternoon, stood on their porches and watched solemnly as the priest got in his car and drove away.

Janet and Jack could not contain their optimism. They went

inside the house, sniffed the air, looked around. Once again it felt as if the house was theirs and did not belong to the demon.

For the duration of daylight and well into the night, their optimism would prove well founded.

On the drive back to Connecticut, enjoying the deep green spectacle of summer along Interstate 84, Father McKenna found himself thinking about an exorcism he'd participated in some years earlier and wondered why he hadn't thought of this before.

In the Brenner case, excavation workers who'd been digging up a drainage ditch had found bones wrapped in decayed cloth buried deep in the ground. Father McKenna had a forensic expert examine the bones. The forensics man determined that they were pig bones at least 800 years old. Immediately, Father McKenna knew why the Brenners' house was haunted. Part of its yard was the site where a pagan ritual had taken place more than eight centuries earlier. No wonder demons infested the house.

As he drove, Father McKenna had the sinking feeling that the exorcism he'd just performed had not worked

Many times, following such a rite, he felt elation, but now he was filled with brooding. He could recall few infestations that had presented the problems the Smurls were encountering, and the priest felt that he had failed to help them.

That night Father McKenna phoned the Smurls to see how things were going. He was half surprised to hear Janet say, "They're going just great, father. And we want to thank you again."

"No problems, then?"

"None at all. We went out and got a pizza to celebrate, in fact."

"Well, I'll be praying for you, Janet."

"Thanks so much, father."

That night as he said his nightly prayers, a tremor of fear

passed through the priest. He had a terrible sense that not all was well at the Smurl household.

Once again a sense of failure flooded through him. He felt almost as if he had somehow betrayed this fine family.

He closed his eyes and continued to pray.

THE APPRENTICE DEMONOLOGIST:

"You wear clothes you don't mind getting dirty because even though the movies like to make believe that our job has a lot of hocus-pocus stuff to it, what we really do is look in crevices, in cracks, in closets, in cellars, in attics, and down chimneys and down wells and down sewers—anywhere dark that things could hide, because that's the kind of place that demons and spirits favor.

"And instead of crystal balls and fancy robes and magic wands we carry tape recorders and flashlights and penlights and screw drivers and putty knives and hammers and even tweezers in some cases, and on top of that we take along video equipment and cameras that can shoot in the dark if necessary and logs in which to note the exact time, and we take along assistants who give us courage and who let us give them courage because they know we're all part of the team."

David Wilson was in his third month as a student of demonology and Ed Warren was helping him prepare for the day that was coming soon—the day David Wilson would quit looking at slides and listening to tapes and would, for himself, enter a house infested with demons.

After talking about the instruments and tools demonologists use, Ed looked at David and said, "Now I want to tell you about some people I know. Some people we're going to be visiting soon."

David Wilson: "Just by his tone of voice, I knew that Ed had finally decided to take me along. I'd expected my first feeling to be one of real joy. But instead, I have to admit, I felt my stomach knot up and I felt my heartbeat increase. There was no doubt about it—as much as I wanted to be a demonologist, going into an infested house still scared me."

At that point Ed proceeded to tell David all about this couple named Janet and Jack Smurl.

The Terrible Truth

*T*hat night, Jack had some problems getting to sleep. Excitement caused him to feel almost supercharged with energy.

The house was calm and quiet. His parents had reflected this welcome turn of events. He hadn't seen them smile so much in nearly two years.

Jack lay in the shadows of the bedroom trying to ease himself into sleep. He thanked God for all his blessings, and within ten minutes found the darkness that was sleep and let it overwhelm him gently.

Jack came up out of bed as if a shotgun blast had sounded in the hallway. He was bathed in sweat and shaking.

Moments later, Janet sat up next to him.

"My God," she said.

They both heard banging in the walls.

A sure sign that it had not gone at all.

After a time, as the banging continued, Janet and Jack went

in to comfort their daughters. The girls were well aware of what the banging represented.

Heather, through tears, said, "Is it ever going to leave us alone, mom? Ever?"

Speaking in barely a whisper, and fighting back her own tears, Janet said, "I don't know, honey. I really don't know."

After an hour or so the banging stopped. The girls went back to sleep.

Jack and Janet lay in bed, wrapped in each other's arms, watching dawn smudge the window.

They were exhausted, drained. And terrified.

"I don't know what we're going to do," Janet said.

"Somewhere there's somebody who can help us. There's just got to be." He went on to say something he thought he'd never say. "Maybe it's time we went public. Maybe somebody will hear us and call us."

"But the girls—"

"Maybe there's some way we can do this anonymously."

"But how?"

"Let's talk to Ed and Lorraine about it."

"Going public is almost as frightening as dealing with the demon," Janet said.

He sighed, stared glumly at the streaked dawn sky. "We've got to do something, Janet. We've got to." But as he thought of all the problems publicity would inflict on his family, Jack said, "Let's give it a little more time. Let's just see what happens. All right?"

Janet said gently, "All right, Jack. If that's what you think is best."

She held him and finally they drifted into uneasy sleep.

Father McKenna's sleep was also troubled that night. He found himself spending many long hours saying ancient prayers for the Smurls, prayers the early Christians believed were the only real weapons against Satan.

Bright Evil

*J*anet and Jack had been asleep only a few minutes when the mattress started shaking.

Jack: "I've never been in an earthquake but I've heard them described, and this was what our bed felt like. Then it started to rise from the bed—the whole mattress—and us with it. Both of us had been levitated before during the haunting but not like this— not with the bed being thrown around so violently. Then, just as usual, we were dropped back onto the frame. I did the only thing I could. As soon as the bed stopped shaking, I grabbed a jar of holy water and started to sprinkle the whole bed. We didn't sleep the rest of the night."

On the Friday of that same week, the Smurl family sat down to the dinner table only to see the oak hutch in the kitchen open by itself. Eighteen cups and saucers came tumbling out and crashed to the floor. Bits and pieces of ruined china were scattered all over the floor, and some of the sharp edges put scratch marks on the bottom of the hutch.

Janet buried her hands in her face and began to weep softly. She had waited seventeen years for the hutch, until they had the money they needed to afford it. And now it was scratched and marred.

Suddenly, anger overtook her, and she raised her head and shouted, "I hate this house!"

Jack and the children spent the next twenty minutes trying to comfort her.

Over the next week the bathroom, which seemed to hold a special appeal for the demon, became very active with examples of infestation, most of it directed toward Janet.

On Monday night, as she stepped into the tub, she saw a large bright human form standing in the corner. It was approximately five feet tall, and looked like a bright light with shoulders and a head, but no neck, legs, or arms. It had no features that Janet could see. Its golden glow hurt her eyes, as if she were gazing directly into the sun.

Terrified, she called out for Jack, but by the time he reached the bathroom, the glowing creature was gone.

On Wednesday, as she sat in the tub, she heard a man moaning "Oh . . . oh . . . oh," as if in sexual ecstasy.

Janet screamed for Jack immediately.

This time Jack stayed with Janet, sitting beneath the crucifix that was over the doorway in the hall. While she finished her bath, he read from a missal. As he read the holy words about the Blessed Mother, Jack and Janet smelled the scent of roses in the air.

Janet: "I don't have any doubt that the forces from heaven were in the house at that moment to wage war against the demon and to protect our family from physical harm."

Unquestionably, the most alarming incident took place that Thursday night, and once more in the bathroom.

Janet went to sleep early but awakened around 2:00 A.M.

Thirsty, she got up to get herself a drink of water. She was tired enough that she didn't give any thought to supernatural beings. She simply wanted a drink of water and then wanted to go back to sleep.

Because of all the incidents lately, Jack had insisted in leaving the bathroom light on all night.

Now, as Janet turned into the bathroom, she saw something that woke her up completely.

Standing in front of the towel cabinet was the large, hunched, hooded black form that had materialized many times since the house had first been infested.

Janet watched, fascinated and repelled at the same time, as the form's hands tried to open the cabinet doors.

Seeming to hear her, the figure's head turned to the right and gazed sightlessly at Janet.

Janet: "I felt as if the thing was looking right through me. My skin literally crawled. I realized that I had only a nightgown on and I was worried about it becoming an incubus and raping me. Then it started to move away from the cabinet and toward me. I ran down the hall, stumbling on a throw rug and banging my knee pretty badly, but I kept running. I went in and started shaking Jack. I was afraid the demon might have put him in a psychic sleep. Fortunately, I was able to wake him up right away. He went with me to the bathroom, taking the holy water along. But by that time the dark form had left. I didn't sleep the rest of the night."

Her fears about the incubus were realized the next night when Janet, relaxing next to Jack on their bed, felt an invisible hand move up her body.

Jack, seeing that his wife was being attacked, grabbed the holy water from the nightstand. After pulling the covers off Janet, he said, in a commanding voice, "In the name of Jesus Christ, I order you to leave!"

Then Janet picked up the same prayer. "In the name of Jesus Christ, I order you to leave!"

The unseen hands continued to violate her but as they sprayed holy water and uttered the words of the special prayer, Janet eventually felt the hands withdraw, her body her own again. Finally, she collapsed in Jack's strong and protective embrace.

But the night was not over.

After getting to sleep an hour later, the Smurls were awakened by the mattress being shaken violently, much as it had earlier. Invisible punches came next, though tonight they lasted only briefly.

But the demon was not done.

It picked up the whole mattress and levitated it about a foot in the air, tilting it up and down like a roller coaster. By the time the demon was finished with them this time, their daughters stood in the doorway, crying and praying.

Janet cried out, "This is our house, damn it. Leave us alone!"

Around three that same morning Janet was visited by an apparition of an elderly woman with a pleasant face. Her hair was pulled back into a bun. She wore wire-rim glasses with round lenses. Beneath a navy blue cardigan sweater she wore a faded house dress. She sat at a phantom of a white, colonial-style table. The woman said nothing to Janet, only smiled at her in her pleasant way.

Janet: "I had the distinct impression this woman wanted to tell me something but I wasn't sure what. We just watched each other. The odd thing was, I wasn't afraid. If this was the demon taking a new form, it had taken a form that didn't frighten me. Then she was gone, table and all, just like that. In her place were these lights—blue, gold, and white—flashing all over, sort of like strobe lights from the sixties. Jack didn't wake up during any of this. I got to sleep just before dawn and then the phone rang. It woke Jack up. He got it but there was nobody on the other end. I told him what had happened with the elderly woman. Neither of us could understand it. Usually the spirits were ugly or scary. This one had been . . . reassuring, I guess."

Next morning, Janet was in the kitchen doing dishes when she heard a noise on the front porch.

Walking into the living room, Janet saw a woman who was a golden, glowing form even more blinding than the creature the other night. The woman's hair, skin, and clothes were composed of this stunning white gold color. Janet couldn't discern any physical features at all. As Janet cautiously approached the door, the woman, predictably, vanished.

That afternoon, doing some cleaning, Janet looked up and saw the same white gold woman standing in front of her. Turning off the vacuum cleaner, Janet started toward the woman, but the woman disappeared once more.

Later in the afternoon, the woman appeared once more. This time, the golden glow seemed to have a fiery essence, and Janet sensed for the first time that the woman was here not merely to alarm her but to hurt her.

In bed that night, Janet turned to Jack to say something to him and she saw, for the first time, her husband look at her as if *she* were the demon.

Jack: "I hadn't been expecting it. We were just having a normal conversation, I mean; and Janet turned to me and then steam started coming from her mouth. It really scared me. I started moving away from her and then I realized that this was exactly what the demon would want me to do. It had forced steam out of Janet's mouth to force us apart. I thought of what Ed and Lorraine had told us about the demon always trying to destroy families. Well, that's exactly what it was doing. So I very calmly told Janet what was happening—about the steam coming out of her mouth—and then she started watching herself and seeing the steam, too. In a way it was sort of funny—we even laughed about it a little—but when I first saw it, it really spooked me. No doubt about that."

In the middle of the night, Jack reached over and touched Janet softly and said, "You awake?"

"Yes."

"It's time, isn't it? To talk to Ed and Lorraine."

"About going public?"

"Yeah."

Janet thought a moment. "I guess at this point I don't know what else we *can* do."

"Maybe somebody out there will know something about cases like this."

As they talked, they heard a cry come from one of the girl's bedrooms.

They ran down the hall and into the twins' room.

Carin was sitting up, tears rolling down her cheeks.

"I saw him again, mommy. I saw him again."

"Who, honey?"

"The man in the long black thing."

"The black cloak?"

"Yes."

Jack and Janet glanced at each other nervously. "What was he doing?"

"He was in the hall. I was afraid he was coming down to your room. To get you."

She started crying again.

Jack, infuriated, slammed a fist into his hand and went back to bed while Janet stayed and comforted Carin.

The demon was beginning to achieve its goal. It was trying to destroy the Smurl family one by one. There was just one thing it hadn't counted on and that was Jack Smurl himself. Nobody was going to destroy Jack's family. Nobody.

ED WARREN:

Father McKenna's sense that the demon had not been overcome by the second exorcism proved to be true.

Lorraine, Chris, and I (and at various times, other members of the team) stayed in contact with Janet and Jack, offering them advice and any solace we could, which, I have to admit, wasn't much at this point, the demon seeming to be virtually if not literally out of control.

One subject that came up many times was the rather ominous one of Amityville, which was a perfect example of what could happen when a demon reached the fourth stage of infestation, that being possession. At Amityville, of course, twenty-four-year-old Ronald DeFeo had taken a rifle and systematically murdered his parents, two brothers, and two sisters. Today he is in prison, sentenced for life.

Until the murder Ronald DeFeo had been a normal young man, filled with the desires of most young men. But some sinister force in the Amityville house had taken control of him and the sad and bloody results have since been well documented.

Lorraine and I spent many long days and nights after being called into the Amityville case trying to determine if Ronald had merely gone insane or if he'd become demon-infested himself. All the evidence, and it was considerable, pointed to the latter. And we're still learning things about the Amityville situation that only strengthen our belief that it was a clear and classic case of possession.

Now, we began to worry along the same lines about the Smurls.

What if the demon took control of someone in the house and turned an otherwise innocent mind to dark and violent thoughts, much as Ronald DeFeo's mind had been turned to dark and violent thoughts?

Father McKenna had done all he could and so had we, and yet the demon and its attendant spirits still prowled both sides of the duplex in West Pittston, its ultimate goal becoming more and more obvious.

It wanted to destroy the Smurl family by whatever means necessary.

One option we considered was getting a group of priests involved in the situation and seeing if, in a collective way, we could derive some plan or insight that would drive the demon from the household.

To be blunt—and I say this as a most devout Catholic—we had no luck whatsoever in interesting the church in helping us. Diocese officials are often skeptical of the supernatural because they fear being drawn into a hoax or something that will later be explained away by perfectly logical means.

About this time, Janet and Jack were getting desperate. They phoned once to say that they were strongly considering selling the house and they phoned another time to say that they were now about to simply abandon their home. We told them the terrible truth. We explained that the demon could well follow them, just as it had to the campground on at least two other occasions, and we also told them that they might buy a new house only to find that the demon lurked in the attic or basement or even kitchen. We convinced them there was nothing to gain in moving.

Janet seemed particularly—and understandably—depressed by this conversation because Jack's sister, Betty Ann Yanovitch, had arrived at the Smurl house with her husband and teenage son Billy. Betty had had a horrible supernatural experience in Janet's house: While using the bathroom, the light on, she had become entirely surrounded by darkness, as if at the bottom of some deep abyss. She remained in the abyss so long she wondered if she wouldn't lose her mind. Finally, the darkness lifted and she saw the bathroom again. The demon once more demonstrated its power, just as it had a few days earlier when Chris Moughan, a nephew, had seen a black figure standing on Jack's and Janet's front porch.

Janet said, "We've been talking, Ed. We think it's time we went public. Maybe when the diocese hears our story, they'll be forced into helping us."

It was the sort of decision neither Lorraine nor I could make for them. It was the sort of decision—a very serious one that might well have a great lasting impact on their lives and the lives of their children—that we had to let them reach on their own.

"You're sure?" I asked.

"Yes," Janet said.

"You realize if word gets out, you could be—"

"Laughingstocks?" She finished the sentence for me. "Nothing could be worse than what we've been going through the past few weeks, Ed. Go ahead. See if you can figure out the best way to make our story public."

By "public" Janet meant the public at large. By now many people in West Pittston knew about the Smurls and their tragic dilemma, and in general, most had reacted sympathetically.

But it has been our experience that when the public is confronted with something it both fears and misunderstands—think back to what Martin Luther King had to endure; or what AIDS patients must go through today—it can be a fickle and vicious judge of others.

I said again, "You're sure this is what you want, Janet?"

There was a pause, but only a slight one, and Janet Smurl said, "Yes, yes I'm sure."

In Philadelphia there's a television talk show called "People are Talking," hosted by an intelligent and open-minded man named Richard Bey. He had already invited Lorraine on, so we called him and asked if we could bring the Smurls along. We promised him that his viewers would be intrigued and shocked by what they had to say. Bey agreed and so we set down certain conditions. Both Lorraine and I still had reservations about the Smurls revealing their identities, so we got Richard Bey's promise that they would be presented behind a screen so that they could not be recognized by viewers. And so that no one would know their last names, we would refer to them only as Janet and Jack. Bey agreed to all our conditions and plans were set for our TV appearance.

THE APPRENTICE DEMONOLOGIST:

The basement door was closed. David Wilson listened as, near the front of Jack and Janet Smurl's duplex, Ed and Lorraine Warren moved around with two other members of the psychic team.

Now, as David smelled spices from a rack over the stove (nutmeg was especially pleasant), his eyes moved to the doorknob and he wondered if he should have volunteered for this assignment, after all.

While both Ed and Lorraine had been in the basement earlier today, and while Lorraine had received many clear psychic impressions of the place and found it safe, David felt anxious about going back down there alone.

He smiled weakly at his fear: This was a lot different from lying on your bed in your parents' home and eating Fritos and reading a book about the occult.

In the five months he'd been preparing for this day, David had seen several people drop out of the program. He'd even seen a strapping big military man reduced to tears after spending long hours in a house heavily infested with malevolent spirits.

As David stood there, he heard the floor creak. In the twilight, the kitchen was gauzy with darkness and the sound of the aged boards made him start.

He spun around, his mind racing with all sorts of dark and frightening images, to find Ed Warren standing there.

"How you doing, David?"

"Oh, fine," David said, swallowing heavily.

Ed grinned. "Were you kind of afraid about going down there?"

"I volunteered," David said.

Ed continued grinning. He put his hand on David's shoulder. "Doesn't mean a fellow can't be scared, just 'cause he volunteers, I mean."

Now David grinned. "I always thought I'd be brave."

"Believe me, you are brave. Otherwise you wouldn't be in this house at all."

David's gaze fell back on the worn metal doorknob.

Ed said, "I'd be glad to go with you."

David silently thanked the older man but then stopped himself. He'd been waiting for this moment for so long, and now he was going to spoil it for himself. Or was he?

"I think it'd be better if I went down there myself," David said.

"You sure?"

David nodded.

"OK," Ed said. "Lorraine and I are going upstairs." He started to turn, then paused. "You positive?"

"Positive."

Ed's easy grin appeared once more. "Gotta admit I'm glad you're doing it alone."

David laughed. "Why don't you come downstairs in about half an hour and tell me that?"

"Hell," Ed said. "I'll even bring you a cup of hot chocolate."

"I'd appreciate that," David said.

Then all that was left was to go down the basement steps just as he'd been planning all along.

Alone.

He set up a tape recorder and set the tape to rolling and then he took out his log book and started making notes on what he saw. He accounted for his time in five-minute increments.

Twice he heard noises he couldn't explain and he jerked up from the straight-backed chair in which he sat, but when he shone his light around, he found nothing unusual or untoward.

Then, as best he could, he sat back down and tried to relax.

The basement smelled of sudsy laundry water and sweet fabric softener. In one of the small oblong windows you could see dirt along the bottom of the glass and in another you could catch a fragment of the night sky and golden clouds racing across the quarter moon.

After a time, he took out his flashlight and began a thorough examination of the basement, every corner, every crevice, every possible place a spirit could use as an entry point or hiding place. He catalogued each of these carefully.

He was on his hands and knees when he heard something that sounded like a piece of chalk scraping across a blackboard. He jumped up so quickly that he banged his head against the side of the washer, hard enough that he nearly knocked himself out.

While holding his left hand against a lump quickly forming on his forehead, he squinted out of one eye to see what had caused the noise.

And that's when he saw that the sound was coming from the dryer, some malfunction of the motor.

And that's how Ed Warren, coming down the stairs with the promised cup of hot chocolate, found him: sitting on the floor, holding his head. From a self-inflicted wound.

"What happened to you?"

"You don't want to know," David said.

Ed looked worried.

David felt obliged to tell him. "I got injured and it wasn't even a spirit," David said, concluding his story.

Ed helped him up and gave him his hot chocolate. Then Ed pointed at the watch on his own thick wrist. "Yeah, but you know what?"

"What?" David said, still smarting from the pain.

"You did what you said you wanted to do. You wanted to stay down here half an hour by yourself and that's just what you did." But even though Ed's voice swelled with pride for David's accomplishment, he sensed that the young man was deeply disturbed.

"I learned something while I was down here," David said.

Though he knew what David was about to say, Ed kept his face free of any expression. He simply let the young man talk.

"I—I'm not cut out to be a demonologist, Ed. It's just too . . . frightening is the only word I can think of. Down here I sensed things I'd just as soon forget. I—"

Ed put a steadying hand on David's shoulder. "You don't need to justify yourself to me, David. You're not the first person to make that decision and obviously you won't be the last."

"I just feel so damn ashamed, I guess."

Ed laughed. "Ashamed of what? Of not wanting to spend your life searching in dark nooks and crannies for demons? You think that's something to be ashamed of?" He nodded to the stairs. "You feel like going out for a pizza?"

"You kidding?"

Ed smiled. "I've never been known to kid about pizza."

Today, David Wilson is employed by a large multinational corporation, is married, and still has nightmares about his half hour in the basement. "It's not something your mind ever lets go of. I know it sounds corny but I was in the presence of true evil and it really shook me, just paralyzed me, in a way. I knew then why so few people stay in the field of demonology. It just takes too much out of you."

An Eerie Trip

Heather, Shannon, and Carin stayed at home with John and Mary Smurl, Dawn visited the Yanovitchs in New Jersey, and early on a Tuesday evening Janet and Jack got into their van and set off for Philadelphia along the beautiful Pennsylvania turnpike.

The month was July and the rolling hills were a furious green.

Jack: "It started out being very relaxing. We were very nervous about what we were going to do—tell our story on TV and all—but we found the trip itself real pleasant. The scenery was great and it was a chance for us to be alone and just talk about normal things. Then something started kicking me in the back."

Jack felt the pressure of a boot grinding into his backbone. The kick was so hard that he was knocked forward into the steering wheel. To keep the car from going off the road, he had to slow down and grip the wheel tightly.

Janet could see that Jack was suddenly drenched in sweat and that his face had become pale. "Something's kicking me!"

Without a word, Janet reached for the holy water she carried in an aspirin bottle. She quickly sprinkled the back seat of the van, then spoke the words of the prayer the Warrens had taught them.

Almost immediately the kicking stopped.

"I guess it doesn't want us to tell our story. Janet said.

Jack surprised her by smiling. "Good, then I'm glad we're doing it."

But the incident in the van would not be their only demonic experience that day.

Once they reached Philadelphia, Janet and Jack checked into a Holiday Inn. They had a good dinner in a nearby restaurant, then went back to their room.

They had been lying down for twenty minutes when the mattress began shaking violently. By now they were well familiar with this particular form of haunting. Holy water, dispensed in great dollops by Janet, brought the shaking to a stop, at least for the time being.

Around midnight the presence began pounding on the mattress with such forceful blows that Janet and Jack had no choice but to sit in chairs and smoke cigarettes, just watching the demon go berserk.

From down the hall Janet could hear the laughter of two couples who were returning to their rooms, slightly drunk and having a good time.

How simple my life used to be, she thought.

She watched the obscene force continue to pummel the mattress.

"We'll be so tired we won't make any sense on TV," Janet said.

Somberly, Jack replied, "I think that's exactly what it's got in mind, honey."

In the morning the Smurls were exhausted and depressed. Not even in a motel far from home could they get a good night's sleep.

ED WARREN:

Lorraine had been fighting a head cold all week so when we met the Smurls for breakfast, about all she felt like eating was a poached egg and a piece of toast.

The dining room was the sort you see in most modern motels, well appointed if you like furniture that is pressed wood rather than real wood, and rather grand in design. Lorraine had once joked that she thought motels hired "madames to do their interior decoration." I had to agree with her.

The Smurls looked bad, nervous and weary, and after they described their night I certainly understood why. They sat across from us in the dining room playing with the breakfast rather than eating it and sounding as if they were having second thoughts about going on the show.

Peripherally, I saw what happened to Lorraine but at first I didn't understand the significance of what was going on.

Janet, startled, said, "It's in here."

And so it was.

Our chairs sat with their backs to a blank wall, yet here was some unseen entity lifting Lorraine's chair half an inch from the floor and smashing it into the table.

I groped in my pocket for holy water and immediately began uttering the prayer that was never far from my lips. Lorraine, long accustomed to the manifestations of the beast, looked anxious, taking my hand as I continued to pray.

The entity left us then. You could feel it withdraw, the air less disturbed, its presence shrinking and then disappearing.

Lorraine smiled bravely. "I'd say there's somebody we've made very angry."

The Smurls tried to smile, too, but they managed only the barest of responses. Their demeanor did not bode well for our appearance on Richard Bey's TV show.

* * *

Working in most modern TV studios is a bit like working aboard a submarine. Massive doors seal you into an environment that is dark except for small areas illuminated by great blasts of light. People move like phantoms in these deep shadows, carrying clipboards and wearing headphones.

Being in the studio only made Janet and Jack more frightened.

The set resembled that of most modern talk shows. We were put in the center of the stage area, while host Richard Bey sat on the edge of the lighted circle. Janet and Jack faced the audience directly, though they were concealed behind a gauzy screen.

Before the show began, Bey talked to the Smurls, obviously trying to reassure them that, given the lighting setup, nobody at home would be able to see their faces.

For the first time in hours, Janet laughed. "Isn't this how they interview Mafia people?"

"In the shadows, you mean?" I asked.

She nodded.

I grinned back. "Now that you mention it, it is."

Richard Bey is known as a tough interviewer. Not excessive—never malicious or petty—but his questions are "hardball" as opposed to "softball."

Well-dressed, tanned, confident, Bey managed to seem genuinely interested in the plight of the Smurls while remaining skeptical about some of their experiences.

He asked the questions his viewing audience would. How did the Smurls know that their experiences couldn't be explained by natural causes? Were they a troubled family and therefore given to the kind of quiet hysteria you find in broken or damaged homes? Had they ever sought professional help—i.e., psychiatric help—to help them deal with the phenomena that were plaguing them?

These were the sort of questions people like the Smurls always got at the beginning of an interview.

But after about ten minutes something very curious started to happen. Before, Bey and the audience alike had been given to occasional uncomfortable titters and laughs, but as Janet and Jack began to talk at length about everything from the mysterious black form that moved from one side of the house to the other, about Jack's rape, about Shannon being hurled down the stairwell, gradually you could see a change in both Bey and the audience.

Where before they'd been skeptical, now they were rapt and serious.

Lorraine and I corroborated what the Smurls were saying. To the inevitable question of why the Smurls didn't simply move, I interjected an experience of my own. I explained that once when I was in England I'd tape-recorded a demon, the horrid voice on the tape telling me exactly what my wife who was 3,000 miles away in Connecticut was doing. I assured the audience, "Preternatural entities, which are negative ones, transcend distance and time and can follow people where ever those people go." To confirm this, I pointed out that the demon had followed the Smurls to Philadelphia and had ruined their night in the motel room.

Then Janet and Jack talked about the two exorcisms. The audience seemed especially fascinated by this subject. They asked if the rites had been anything like the movie *The Exorcist.* Janet and Jack explained how the movie had been exaggerated for dramatic effect.

While they were talking, Father McKenna phoned in and addressed the studio audience. He talked about why some of his exorcisms worked and some didn't. Though he could not prove this contention, he said, it was his belief that the religious rites may have been unsuccessful because of some occult items buried in the ground beneath the Smurls' home.

During the entire interview, Janet expressed bitterness only once, and that's when the subject of the Catholic Church came up. She said that the family had received virtually no help from the church. Lorraine agreed, saying it was sad the way some churches treat families that are haunted, and she urged that church officials spend more time helping families instead of being doubtful.

Richard Bey asked me, "Are demons afraid of anything?"

"Only one thing, really, Richard. The power of God."

"Can you summon up that power?"

"Through prayer you can."

Bey, smiling, said that after all these years of being psychic investigators, we probably weren't Satan's favorite people.

I said, "He knows who we are. In many hauntings we've heard our names called out."

"Does that frighten you?"

Lorraine said, "Of course it does, Richard. Of course it does."

Then Bey wondered aloud if demons haunted friends of the Smurls who'd been in the house.

Janet said, "Unfortunately, yes." Then she related several of the more unnerving experiences of friends of theirs.

Finally, it was time for questions from the audience.

One woman, obviously upset, said, "Could demons follow any of us in the audience home?"

Nervous giggles.

"It's possible," I said, "but probably unlikely." I went on to tell them that simply by discussing demons here we were giving the dark world recognition. "So," I said, "I envisioned the entire audience in Christ's light before the show began, just in case."

Another woman in the audience talked of an experience she'd had with a Ouija board and how it had told her she was going to hell. Lorraine promptly cautioned the audience and viewers about using Ouija boards, and said that in the majority of the cases she and I investigate, people had invited the demons in by first communicating with the supernatural world through such tools as the boards.

There were other audience questions and, as always, we found that those who'd come to scoff turned out to be the most interested of all in the twin subjects of supernatural and paranormal phenomena.

Janet and Jack never relaxed, however. Lorraine and I kept looking in their direction and smiling. You have to appreciate what they were going through. They'd had a terrible night and now they were being asked to reveal some of their most intimate secrets for a television audience. It wasn't the kind of soul-searching most of us would want to do in public.

Richard Bey's final question was the most somber one of all. He asked what I thought was the ultimate goal of the demon.

I answered him simply. "It wants to destroy the Smurl families."

"Why?"

"In our experience, we've found that diabolical forces hate loving families. The Smurls live in the image of God and this the demon finds totally repugnant. So it wants to destroy them."

Bey wanted to know if we could stop the demon.

"I'm hopeful we can," I said.

I wish my words had sounded more confident and purposeful but given all that had happened over the last few months, and thinking back to some of our other cases, I knew that occasionally demons did triumph for a time, until psychic investigators and ordained members of the clergy could figure out deterrents.

The show finished, the audience gave the Smurls long and warm applause, and I could see in the tired faces of the couple something like gratitude.

Afterward, Janet said, "The audience was very nice to us."

Lorraine said. "They knew you were telling the truth and they respected you for it."

Jack said to me, "What do we do next?"

"All we *can* do is wait and see what happens. We need to be in constant contact on the phone."

Janet said, her eyes misting over, "Right now. I'd just like to see our kids."

Lorraine leaned over and kissed her on the cheek. "That sounds like a good idea. Why don't you leave now? You can be home before suppertime."

From the parking lot, we waved good-bye, smiling all the time.

But when we were alone I said, "I wish I felt better about this."

"I know," Lorraine said. "I know. I'm almost afraid of what's going to happen in the next few days. If the demon was angry enough to follow them here—"

She didn't have to finish the sentence.

The Demon Retaliates

*F*or the next two weeks, life at the Smurl duplex in West Pittston became nearly intolerable.

Just as the Warrens feared, the haunting increased in ferocity.

Mary: "The day Janet and Jack appeared on the TV show was one of the worst days ever on our side of the house. The banging got so loud at one point that we actually had to leave the house. Finally, the noise quieted down enough that we could go back inside with the girls, but then the banging started up on Janet and Jack's side. It was loud enough that it kept us up all night."

John: "That same day I started experiencing the psychic colds again. It was like something was drawing the heat from my body. I remember shivering so hard that I was afraid my teeth were going to crack. I was worried about Mary, too. Given her heart condition, the doctor said the worst thing that could happen to her was constant stress, and that's what we were all under. Constant, constant stress."

* * *

Three nights later, asleep, Janet Smurl sensed the covers being eased sinuously off her body and cast on the floor.

As her eyes started to flutter open and her head began to rush with a disorienting feeling of losing control of her body, she saw that she was now suspended in midair.

What was even more startling was that, in a perfectly prone position, she was being floated across the room.

As if she were undergoing some lighter-than-gravity experience, she bumped into the bedroom wall, then bounced away.

Then the demon quit having fun with her and hurt her viciously.

Janet: "Obviously it's not something I'll ever forget. It twisted me around several times and then hurled me into the far wall. Just before I crashed, I crossed my hands over my skull to protect it from the collision. Then the demon turned me over very quickly and at such an angle that my hands and arms were outstretched. I only had a few seconds to put myself into the fetal position because I could see the demon was going to catapult me again into the wall, this time trying to break my hands and arms. All the time this was happening, I was screaming for Jack to wake up, really pleading with him, but of course the demon had seen to it that Jack was in a deep psychic sleep. What happened finally I can't even really describe. All I could think of was being in a trance. I saw everything in our shadowy bedroom very clearly but at the same time I had the sense that I was caught between worlds, this one and the life after, almost as if I was hanging between life and death itself—and then suddenly I was lying next to Jack and I was sobbing, really out of control, and he woke up and tried to calm me down, asking me what had happened, and I showed him the bruises from where the demon had slammed me into the wall, and then I went back to sobbing again. I was afraid I'd really been pushed over the edge. You know the feeling? When you just can't handle things anymore? That's how I was. I really couldn't deal with things anymore."

* * *

Jack's test on the edge would come the following night.

Jack: "The kids knew what had happened to their mother, being levitated and all, so they let her rest all day and did all the housework themselves and even helped with dinner. They could see how precarious her health was getting. I told her to call Ed and Lorraine while I was at work, just to keep her calm. Well, she did, and talking to them helped a lot. When I got home we had dinner and watched a little TV. Janet was exhausted, drained, so we put the kids to bed early and then sacked out early ourselves. According to the digital clock I was asleep about a half hour before I heard the thing."

The "thing" Jack referred to was a creature roughly eight feet in height that stood on two legs but had, on top of its wide shoulders, a furry head with blinding red eyes and a piglike snout. Standing at the end of the bed, the creature slavered and slobbered, then clawed at the air with rakelike fingers, seeming to threaten Jack with evisceration. Even more repugnant than the shape of the creature's face was the slobbering noises of its lips, which resembled pieces of liver, as they took in air and saliva.

Janet: "Jack's scream woke me up and almost instantly I started screaming, too, even though by then the creature he described was gone. I'd never seen Jack that shaken by anything before. He'd thrown himself off the bed and lay in a ball in the middle of the floor. In the moonlight you could see that his whole body was covered in sweat. His hands were in fists that he kept pounding against the floor. I couldn't tell which emotion was stronger in him, fear or anger. The whole family was going through that. We were *tired* of being afraid, yet we didn't want to give in to the demon, either. I went over and lay down on the floor next to Jack and slowly began to run my hands softly up and down his back, trying to calm him down. His breathing was still coming in big, gasping chunks. It took me ten minutes to get him calmed down. Then he said to me, 'Now I know what hell's going to look like.' He tried describing the creature to me again but he'd run out of words that could do the job. I wasn't all that interested in imagining the thing, anyway. I didn't need much convincing that the form the demon had assumed was disgusting—I'd had plenty of my own experience with it. I got Jack in bed and went down the hall and got him a drink of water. When I came back, he had a rosary in his hands. His lips were moving silently in prayer. But it was his eyes I kept staring at. He was still in a kind of shock. Obviously he couldn't forget what he'd just seen. He stayed awake all night, just like that."

Over the next few weeks, several of the Warren team members visited the Smurls and they returned with increasingly bizarre accounts of what life at the Smurl house had become.

♦ Gloria Dmohoski, Janet's mother, on a visit to the Smurl home, heard a voice resembling Jack's calling her, yet when she investigated she found that it was not Jack at all but a voice that appeared from nowhere.

♦ A few days later, Mary Smurl heard a similar voice calling her. Again, when she checked through the house, she found nothing.

♦ The following day Jack was attacked at 2:00 A.M. by invisible forces that scalded his legs with some kind of intense heat. Only holy water doused the searing pain.

♦ Janet and Jack were kept up all night by the phone ringing on and off. This woke and upset the girls, and the couple spent much of the night trying to convince the girls everything was all right.

♦ The next night banging in the walls began again in series of three knocks, a signal from the demon.

♦ The same night around 3:00 A.M. the phone started in again, three rings in each burst, and so the family, including all the girls, simply got out of bed and went down to the kitchen where Janet made everybody sandwiches. Janet found humor in the situation: "What a ridiculous way to have a picnic!" she told her family, as the wall-banging continued.

The next night's incident was not so funny.

The heat being very intense—West Pittston was setting records—Janet and Jack slept wearing very little and with all the covers except the sheet pushed on the floor.

Down the street a dog barked, a motorcycle carrying a young couple out on a late date zoomed down the street, the shadows of heavy maple leaves played against Jack's sleeping form. Janet watched her husband fondly. During the trial of the last few years she'd grown to admire and respect him more than ever.

Janet: "It was while I was lying there getting very sentimental about our relationship that I sensed the mist gathering. It was a very fine mist, almost like an ocean spray, and I felt it before I saw it. I remember trying to touch my face and then I realized that I couldn't move my arm. I was in some kind of hypnotic state. Then the man appeared. He had very bright, almost neon eyes that were a mixture of yellow and green, and two animal horns protruded from his head. Strangely, he also had a very bushy mustache. The mist covered his face so that I could not get a careful look at his features—just the eyes burning in the hollows of his face. I had no doubt what he wanted and I remember wishing I was wearing more clothes. I knew I needed to break through the spell he had cast if I was going to avoid what he wanted from me. Several times I tried calling out but no words came from my throat, and then I said the Hail Mary. I could hear my voice cracking and sounding like a child's, it was so weak, but at least I could hear it. As I said the first words of the Hail Mary, I could see that the creature's eyes glowed with an even deeper hatred of me. Then suddenly, my voice became very loud, I suppose out of desperation, and I saw the creature start to dematerialize. My arm started to function again. I grabbed the bottle of holy water and sprinkled some at the creature and finally it disappeared entirely."

* * *

Jack: "It was time for drastic measures and both of us knew it. We had to look at the up side and the down side. The up side being, of course, that if we went public, revealed our names and identities, somebody might hear our story and contact us with the information we needed to sweep our home clean of the haunting. We hoped that there was somebody else out there who had gone through the same things and might have some wisdom for us. Certainly we couldn't be the only people who'd ever had this sort of supernatural experience. We even felt, as we sat and talked about it, that when the priests at the diocese office heard about it, they would be shamed into helping us. How could they refuse us when our plea was so public? The down side was what we'd feared all along—that once the public heard our story, they would turn against us, see us as lunatics or publicity-seekers. Both Janet and I are proud people, especially where our children are concerned, and we did not want to see them subjected to ridicule and suspicion. But the longer we talked about it, the more we realized we had to do it—go public and see if we could find help—even at the risk of exposing ourselves to ridicule."

ED WARREN:

The Sunday of that week the Smurls called us after having a long meeting in a restaurant at which they decided to really go public with their story—not even hide behind a screen to conceal their faces and identities.

Lorraine and I believed that Janet's and Jack's sudden desire to find a public forum offered one very good possibility—that the Scranton diocese would have to recognize, at last, that something was going on in West Pittston that they had yet to take seriously. I also agreed with Jack, as we spoke that night on the phone, that there was at least the chance that somebody well versed in the history of West Pittston would come forward with a vital piece of information.

I also raised the possibility of more exorcisms.

"More?" Jack said. "Ed, we've had two."

I explained to him that sometimes several exorcisms were necessary, and that we'd been involved with cases where scores of exorcisms had to be performed before diabolical entities were driven from a home.

Then I warned him about the public reaction.

"I know," Jack sighed. "It could be pretty bad."

I chose my next words carefully, not wanting to upset him unduly, but wanting him to understand the gravity of what I was saying. "Public reaction starts to have a life of its own, Jack. Very quickly it can turn into a circus, particularly with the media involved. One day you can be a hero and the next you can be a scoundrel—or a liar. You have to be careful of this, especially when something as volatile as the supernatural is involved." I paused. "I just want you to be aware of this."

"Are you saying not to do it?"

"No, I'm just trying to prepare you. We're friends, Jack."

A silence, then, "We have to do it, Ed. We have to."

For all the arguments I'd given him to the contrary, I knew it was right.

After a supernatural rape and at least two incidents that could justifiably be called life-threatening, and with no apparent end in sight, Janet and Jack had no choice but to take the ultimate risk— the risk of exposing themselves to a fickle and sometimes vicious public.

The Devil Incarnate

Q. Jack, could you tell us what happened the night the beast appeared to you.

A. It wasn't a happy time.

Q. Meaning?

A. [Long silence.] Meaning we were beginning to wonder if *anything* we did would help our circumstances.

Q. Could you explain?

A. Well, this was a few days after we'd decided to go public with our story.

Q. I see.

A. And it was a few weeks after our appearance on television.

Q. Had you had any reaction to your appearance on the Richard Bey show?

A. That was the problem. We'd gotten many sympathetic phone calls—at least none of the kooks called up—but unfortunately no one was able to help us with our problem. About the best they could do was wish us well.

Q. So this was a depressing time?

A. Yes, as you know, the haunting activities had been intense. The dark form appeared in Shannon's room in the middle of the night and we got very worried about her. We couldn't stop her crying. We'd never seen her this grief-stricken. She just couldn't be calmed down, no matter what we said or did.

Q. Did something happen to Dawn, too?

A. Yes. She woke up at five one morning and went downstairs to get a glass of water. On her way down she heard three loud knocks on the front door. She came upstairs to get me but when I got down there, nobody was there. We both went back to bed and then for the next fifteen minutes it really gave Janet and me a show—banging inside the closet, slamming the drawers in the triple dresser, and flipping dresser handles up and down. But then that had been pretty much standard operating procedure for the past few weeks. Following the TV show, it seemed to have this need to reestablish its dominance.

Q. Would you tell us about the incident with Simon?

A. I was lying in bed—Janet was asleep but I was having trouble nodding off—so I just lay there smoking a cigarette in the darkness when I heard Simon beginning to gasp. That's the only way I can describe it. He just couldn't get his breath. This terrible feeling came over me. I love Simon almost as much as I do my own children. I had started to get up from the bed to see what was wrong with him when I felt this presence in bed next to me. Now,

I never saw this presence but I sensed it. There was this huge heartbeat, very regular and very loud, filling the room, and then something gripped my right arm so tight I thought it was going to literally crush it. Then a really fetid odor started to fill my nostrils and I was afraid I was going to pass out. I jerked my left hand toward the nightstand—I can remember the sound of several things being knocked to the floor but I didn't care—and somehow I got the holy water and I sprinkled it across myself and said the prayer that Ed and Lorraine had taught us, and then finally it was gone.

Q. How about Simon?

A. By the time I reached him, he was all right, thank God. He was scared, you could tell that. He was curled up in the corner and still kind of whimpering very low, but when I started petting him he calmed down.

Q. Then you went back to bed?

A. Yes.

Q. And did anything else happen that night?

A. Yes, a little later on, I went down to the bathroom and that's when I saw it. Nothing I'd seen before could have prepared me for it.

Q. Can you describe it for us?

A. I'll try. I wish I was better at this kind of thing. [Pause.] It was huge, for one thing. It had two animal legs—I'd say they resembled a horse's legs—and part of its face was human and part, the snout, I guess, was that of an animal, with black wet nostrils and brown fur over most of its skull and face. It had rounded hips that were covered with fur and eyes that kind of . . . shone, there's no other way to describe it. They shone but at the same time they were human, too. It saw me and slashed at the air with hands—or hooves—that looked partly human and looked partly animal. It

192

made a snorting sound that almost made me nauseous to hear. I got all this in a glimpse as soon as I turned the light on, and almost immediately the creature charged at me. The most threatening thing about it was its sheer size. This thing was at least seven feet tall. All I could think of was that a horse and a human had been grafted together in a real crude way—and then the thing was swiping the air at me.

Q. What did you do?

A. I ran down the hall.

Q. It came after you?

A. Most definitely. Even though our hallway is carpeted, it was running so hard after me that you could hear the stomping sounds its hooves made on the rug.

Q. This sounds something like the creature you'd seen a few weeks earlier.

A. It was—very definitely—but there was something more terrifying about this one.

Q. What did you do?

A. I got into bed and pressed myself back against the headboard and started to reach for the holy water.

Q. Started to?

A. The thing was still slashing at the air.

Q. Then what?

A. Then I grabbed a prayerbook from the nightstand and lifted it toward the creature and then it ran across the bed.

Q. *Across* the bed?

A. Yes. It was real—I could smell it and hear it and feel it running across the bed—but then it just vanished into the wall.

———

Q. You're sure it wasn't a dream?

A. No, because as I sat there—and I was really shaken; I was nearly in tears and no matter what I tried, I couldn't wake Janet up—I could smell its odor in the room. So could Janet when she did wake up.

Q. Didn't that make you think twice about going public?

A. No, in an odd way it made up our minds that going public was the only thing left to us. Because the entity was really going berserk. Mary and John were being bothered again, spending many sleepless nights because of the banging, and then even our neighbors started being hauled into our situation.

Q. Which neighbors were those?

A. Bill and Phyllis Watson.

Statement of
Phyllis Watson

A few months before, strange things began happening to my family—my husband Bill, who is an insurance representative; my twenty-one-year-old daughter Debbie; my sixteen-year-old son Paul. Janet Smurl had told me some of the things that had occurred in her home.

As a licensed practical nurse, I've seen the ravages of mental illness close up—the absolute belief on the part of a psychotic personality that something took place when in fact it didn't.

While I certainly didn't think Janet or anyone in her family was psychotic, her revelations were so odd that I frankly didn't know what to make of them.

These days, because of movies and television, we all have at least a rudimentary understanding of the occult. But what Janet told me was unlike anything I'd seen on a screen. Most of it wasn't as dramatic—in what she'd told me there weren't any monsters per se, but lighting fixtures did drop from the ceiling and terrible odors filled the house, and there was almost constant banging in the walls.

Coming from Janet, who is a very level-headed person, it was all plausible, but still I had to wonder if her imagination hadn't run away with her.

In the summer of 1986 I abruptly and convincingly found out otherwise.

On hot summer nights my husband and I often stay up late and watch TV. Even with all the windows open, the house is too hot for any prolonged sleep. You wake up bathed in sweat.

This particular summer night was setting heat records so we sat in front of the television watching a crime movie and sipping ice tea. It was two in the morning and the movie had just started. The next day was Saturday so we could sleep late. The movie had been running for perhaps five minutes when the screaming started.

At first it was so horrible, it almost sounded faked, by which I mean there's a way women scream in the movies that rarely resembles the way they scream in real life. This sounded more like a movie scream.

The screaming went on for no longer than a minute then faded.

"My God," my husband said, "what was that?"

"I'm not sure," I said.

He got up and went out on the front porch and looked around and came back in. "Didn't see anything."

My heart pounding, we waited a few more minutes before allowing ourselves to get caught up in the movie again.

We'd been watching it another twenty minutes when the screaming came again.

This time it was so piercing and ragged and threatening that it literally lifted me off the couch.

"It's coming from the Smurl house," Bill said.

"But that's impossible," I said. "Janet told me that the whole family was going camping this weekend. We saw them leaving this morning, remember?"

"God, you're right," Bill said. "But what the—"

Then another burst of screaming exploded on the night air. Because our house is about eighteen feet to the left of the Smurls', the sound of the woman shrieking might as well have been coming from our own living room.

Bill went to the side window and looked up at the Smurl house. As the screaming continued he said, "It seems to be coming from Dawn and Heather's room."

And that seemed to be the case. I scanned the Smurl house carefully, listening to the tortured sounds even though they were beginning to really frighten and somehow aggravate me.

"But who could be in there?" I asked.

He reminded me of what Janet had said about the haunting.

All I could think about was ghosts running around in sheets, like children on Halloween, but I knew that what we were dealing with here was real and serious—any maybe even deadly.

Neither of us slept well that night. We kept getting up to check on the children. Instinctively, we seemed to understand that the force operating in the Smurl house—and by now we had no doubt that what Janet had been telling us was absolutely real—might somehow threaten our children.

As soon as Janet and Jack returned, we went over to their duplex and told them about our experience. They shared with us some advice given them by their friends Ed and Lorraine Warren and told us to pray that the entity would not include us in its plans.

A few nights later, Bill and I discovered that the entity had indeed decided to inflict itself on our lives.

Our daughter Debbie is a college student. If the word "normal" can apply to anybody, it most certainly applies to her, spending the bulk of her time in a world of pizza, rock and roll, boys, and, fortunately, a very serious attitude toward her studies.

Around two A.M. I was watching TV after work (I work a late shift and am keyed up when I get home). My husband was asleep in the front bedroom, and Paul was asleep in the middle bedroom. Debbie's bedroom is at the end of the house.

Debbie was awakened by the sound of scratching at the window. The window does not have any trees or bushes around it and is on the second floor. She wondered if somebody might be trying to break in.

Of course, I knew none of this until she came downstairs and said, "There's something in my room, mom. And it's ice cold up there." Then she told me about the scratching.

I didn't know what to make of it so, being protective, I asked her to come over and sit with me. Her fear was catching—I was afraid to go into her room, as well. She sat with me till four or so and then I walked her back to her room. Neither of us slept well that night.

Unfortunately for my daughter, this was not to be her only experience with the supernatural.

A week after the scratching incident, she came running downstairs in her yellow nightgown. She looked to be freezing, her arms folded tightly across her chest, her teeth chattering. I wondered if she'd suddenly gotten a fever.

Debbie: "I'd drifted off to sleep and when I started to wake up I realized that my whole body was covered with goosebumps and was trembling. Sometimes in the winter you kick the covers off yourself while you're asleep and you wake up and you're really freezing. It was like that only worse. My whole body was shaking. I couldn't stop. By the time I got completely awake, it was like I was inside a meat locker. Really. The thing was, this was a very hot summer night. And again I felt this *presence* in the room with me. The temptation was just to lie there because I was still drowsy but I knew that something serious would happen to me if I didn't force myself up out of bed and go find my mother."

When I asked Janet Smurl about Debbie's experience, she told me it was something that had happened to her daughters many times. I also described to Janet other curious things that had been happening—our front door opening and closing by itself in the middle of the night. At first I'd thought it might be our other son, Michael, coming in late, but I went downstairs to have a look and

198

there it was, opening and closing—it happened twice—with no-body in sight.

Of course Janet knew firsthand that my family was getting drawn into the Smurl haunting. My son Paul was at the Smurl house one afternoon with Dawn and her cousin Chris Moughan. Dawn and Chris went into the kitchen, leaving Paul alone in the living room. He sat there several minutes by himself reading a magazine and then he heard tapping sounds coming from the coffee table. He looked under the table but found nothing. He couldn't see anything that could cause such tapping. Gradually, he came to understand that there was a presence in the room. The tapping continued as Dawn and Chris came back into the room. Paul described to Dawn what had been happening. "Don't worry," Dawn said. "You get used to it."

But Paul felt curiously exhausted, drained. Later on Janet explained to me how the entity literally draws on the energy of human beings for sustenance. All I knew when Paul appeared in the doorway telling me of his tapping experience was that my son looked pale and shaken. I put him to bed immediately. He remained exhausted for many hours.

And the haunting continued to be part of our lives: Debbie, on the phone one day, heard the magnetic latch on her clothes closet creak open and then, after several seconds, shut itself again. Debbie felt a being in the room with her. She slammed down the phone and ran from the room, terrified.

Bill: "Sometimes in the summer I like to go for walks when I can't sleep. This one night I did that and when I got home I saw that the Smurl house was completely dark. Then I remembered they were out of town. I started up the steps to my duplex and that's when I heard it—this giant fluttering sound moving from window to window inside the Smurl house. You got the impression that some gigantic bird was trapped inside there and was trying desperately to get out. Then tappings started against the windows, very sharp tappings, almost like gunshots. I don't mind admitting that I didn't stay around for the rest of the show. I ran up the steps and inside my house and closed all the windows and checked the locks on the doors."

Only a Temporary Escape

*T*wo weeks after the phone conversation in which Jack Smurl had told Ed Warren that he and Janet had decided to go public, the Smurls had yet to take any steps that would make their decision a reality.

Jack: "Every time we'd go to pick up the phone and call a newspaper or a TV station, one or both of us would say that maybe we'd better think this over a little longer. Looking back, I'd say we were probably trying to stall until some kind of solution presented itself that wouldn't involve revealing ourselves to the media. The prospect of that was still just about as unnerving as the haunting itself."

Not that Jack didn't keep in close touch with the Warrens during this time. "We talked virtually every day, and what we talked about was an idea I was almost afraid to bring up because it was so radical—but that certainly was my mood at the time. Very radical. I just wanted to be done with the haunting.

"My idea was simple. I asked Ed and Lorraine if they thought it would be a good idea if we had the house torn down and leveled and then moved away. We would suffer great financial losses but at least it might be a new start for us—for all of us, Janet and the kids, and my mother and father as well.

"Now, I knew what Ed would say—that the entity had already proved it could follow us, and had in fact followed us, to the campground, to the motel in Philadelphia, and even to my office.

"However, when I looked at everything carefully, I thought I discerned a certain pattern: that even though the entity followed us, when it left the house, it did not seem to commit acts nearly as atrocious as those it committed inside the duplex.

"So I asked Ed his opinion about us demolishing the house and then moving. And I certainly recall his answer."

Ed: "The day Jack called and said he was thinking of leveling his home, the home he'd worked all his life to own, I knew that the Smurls were at a very dangerous place. In fact, a part of me wondered if the demon hadn't already defeated the family. The other part of the conversation that bothered me was that Jack was desperately pushing for answers that I could not, in all honesty, provide. Would the spirit follow them? Would the spirit be as malicious in a new place? Would the spirit be with them the rest of their lives? In a few previous cases of infestation, we'd seen this kind of despair before, and it's always heartbreaking to behold, particularly when you see it in as good and reliable a man as Jack Smurl. A grave injustice had been done to him and his family and he was asking me—pleading with me, really—for help, any kind of help, now in the form of advice. So that day I did all I could. I said that I did not think that tearing down and leveling his house was a good idea. I said that it would be an expensive and painful process and that there would be no guarantee whatsoever that this would accomplish what he was trying to accomplish. I said that maybe if he thought about it some more a better plan would evolve, one that would not see him destroy something he and his parents were so proud of. Reluctantly, he agreed with me. I have to say that after we hung up, I felt very bad, and Lorraine and I began saying prayers for the Smurl families immediately. We had seen certain families pushed to the brink, and subsequently pushed over that brink. Would that happen to the Smurls? We wondered."

Jack had finished his conversation with Ed that afternoon. The rest of the day, gloomy that none of his ideas were working out, Jack spent in the kitchen making notes about the nearly two years of severe haunting, and seeing if any new plans suggested themselves.

Without his realizing it, dusk came purple in the windows.

Janet, finished with the dinner dishes, sat down with Jack and asked if he wanted to talk. He looked haggard and she was worried about him.

Janet: "We started talking about a number of options, which included renting a place for a time, but we knew the children's lives would suffer and we wondered too what the impact would be on Mary's life. Then there was the prospect of renting a place with new neighbors and having them find out through some incident that we were a supernaturally besieged family. I mean, it would be pretty embarrassing to move into an apartment house and have the people below us hear cloven hooves running up and down the hallway.

"We must have sat there for two hours. The kids got ready for bed and kissed their father goodnight and went upstairs and we just kept on sitting there, talking about what we could do. Every time we thought nothing could get any worse, it would get worse. And right now was a good example. Here was Jack with a week of vacation, and instead of enjoying ourselves, we were in the kitchen brooding about the haunting. And somewhere in there, the idea came to us. I'm not even sure which one of us had the idea first and it doesn't matter. It was just there and it was something we should have thought of earlier, something that would, in effect, be the same thing as razing our duplex, something that would allow us to see just how bad the infestation had become and what would happen if both Smurl families moved out. By dawn the next morning, we had packed up the van and were setting off for the campground. We were laughing, too. We really felt a sense of optimism."

Flight

*T*he experiment both Smurl fami-
lies attempted did not work successfully. Mary Smurl was interviewed at length about it.

Q. Mary, what was the experiment all about?

A. We felt—all of us—that if we all left the entire house
empty for a week, we'd be able to see how the demon would
respond. If it would follow us and, if so, what would it do.

Q. So you felt that if you all went to the campground for a
week and nothing happened, then you'd be safe to move and the
demon wouldn't follow you?

A. Yes.

Q. Were you as optimistic as Janet and Jack?

A. At that point we were ready to try—and maybe even
believe in—just about anything.

Q. So it didn't take much convincing to get you to pack your bags and go along in the van?

A. No convincing at all.

Q. Your husband John felt the same way?

A. Yes. What you have to remember is that within the span of a few short years, we'd been forced to move out of our house in Wilkes-Barre because of the flood and then we'd finally found a place where we could spend our retirement years and—[long pause]—you know what I'm talking about. [Long pause.] All John could say, over and over the week before we left for the campground was, "Why does it want to make us suffer?" He was worried about my health and I was starting to worry about his health, too.

Q. His health was suffering?

A. Well, on TV and in the newspapers you always see material on the relationship between stress and illness, and I think it's hard for most people to understand the kind of stress we'd been under. And I mean constant stress. When somebody talks about a knocking in the wall in print it may not look that threatening. But believe me, when you're sitting in your living room and all of a sudden something begins banging inside your wall, your whole system responds. According to the article, stress damages your immune system. You could see that; all of us were getting colds and flu and headaches. And you certainly didn't have to wonder why.

Q. So you were hopeful that a week at the campground would show you a way of escaping?

A. Yes, even though we'd put all our money into the duplex, we were willing to lose what we had and start over. We felt that if our faith in God was strong enough we'd make it. So that's why we went to the campground. We even made a pact.

Q. A pact?

A. Yes. Janet and Jack and John and I. We said that no matter what happened, no matter where the demon forced us to live, we would continue living together as a family. Janet even said, "If we have to leave our house empty and rent a second place to do that, we will. This thing won't beat us. It *won't.*" It was a very emotional point and John and I both had tears in our eyes.

Q. Can you describe the campground?

A. Oh, it's the sort you see in the Pennsylvania hills, kind of like a little village really, when you put all the campers and their cars together. One problem we had right off was the weather. Black rain clouds hung low in the sky and it was chilly for a summer day.

Q. Were the rain clouds a portent?

A. [Hesitation.] You mean like an omen?

Q. Yes.

A. [Pause.] They could have been.

Q. It didn't go so well at camp?

A. No.

Q. What happened?

A. [Another long pause. It is obvious to the interviewer that Mary is gathering her strength. She has begun to fidget.] The demon attacked my bed in the camper.

Q. Would you describe that for us, please?

A. The bed is nailed to the floor. There is no way you can move it. That first night—it was just after midnight—I was asleep in the camper when I heard very hard and rapid rappings on the roof and floor. I started to get up out of my bed but before I could, I felt the whole bed being ripped from the floor, jerked to the left and then jerked to the right. You could hear the nails tearing at the floor.

Q. Did anybody come to help you?

A. I screamed, of course, but one thing about the demon is its speed. The whole incident was over before anybody could reach me.

Q. It just stopped?

A. It just stopped.

Q. [Mary's fragile health is never more apparent than during this interview. As she speaks, her eyes take on a curiously luminous quality and whatever anger she might have for the demon is dissipated by sheer physical weariness.] What were your feelings then, Mary, about the whole situation?

A. [Long pause.] It was becoming obvious that not only could the demon follow us but it could pretty much do what it wanted to.

Q. How did the week at the campground go from there?

A. [She looks at the interviewer and shakes her head. Her words are barely audible.] From there it only got worse. Much worse.

Q. But hadn't things like this happened when Janet and Jack had visited the campground before?

A. Yes, but what was supposed to be special about this trip was that both families had left the entire house vacant. In a very real sense, we had turned over the house to the demon as a kind of sacrifice. We wanted to see if it would respond by leaving us alone at the campground.

Q. So if it had left you alone—

A. Then we'd realize that what it wanted was something in the house itself and we'd all vacate. We'd do what Janet had said:

"We'll rent if we have to." But we'd move right away and we'd stay together no matter what.

Q. So when the demon tried to tear your bed from the floor, what was the reaction?

A. Well, the first thing was, of course, that everybody was very frightened for me.

Q. What did they feel about the demon in general?

A. Well, even though we all agreed it was too soon to tell how the week would go for sure, we had a pretty good suspicion, I'm afraid, of what lay ahead for us. It turned out to be a terrible week, and I was sorry we had Chris Moughan along because things got pretty tough for everybody. But then we'd had high hopes that it would be a real vacation.

A Troubling
Realization

*T*he time was 3:00 A.M., the third day of the camping trip. Jack lay awake, still thinking about the incident that had taken place around midnight, when he'd gotten up in response to a shout from his father from a sleeping berth near the front of the camper.

"I couldn't believe it," John Smurl had anxiously told his son. "I felt the whole mattress being lifted up from under me. I was afraid it was going to throw me into the wall. Then I looked out the window." John Smurl had shaken his head, exhausted from his encounter with the supernatural. "I saw this white form appear outside the window—I'd have to say it was dressed in chiffon—and it stayed there a moment and then just walked away. Just like that!"

Jack had embraced his father to keep the older man from trembling.

A rage rose in Jack, one he knew well by now, one he had no idea what to do about.

So now it was 3:00 A.M. and he lay awake.

By now, the fourth day of their camp sojourn just ahead of him, he knew the answer to the question he'd come here to find out. Wherever Jack Smurl went, the entity was going to follow.

There in the darkness, moonlight casting long shadows through the camper windows, the scent of wood smoke from the campfire outside pleasant on the air—there in the darkness the entity responded to Jack Smurl's bitterness.

The sound of animal hooves striking the metal roof penetrated the darkness like gunfire.

Jack sat upright, bathed in sweat and wanting to physically attack the unseen force that was tormenting him. He rushed over to the center of the camper to where the holy water was kept. Armed with a vial of the sacred fluid, he stood up and began sprinkling the water across the ceiling. As he did so, he let his eyes rove out to the campsite, to the guttering fire and the leafy summer oaks encircling them.

Sitting on a picnic table bench, looking calm and peaceful like a contented picnicker, was the faceless, cloaked black form that Jack knew to be the demon itself.

An anger he'd never know before—a blinding anger that turned him into a being that was as much animal as man—overtook Jack and he smashed into the camper door so hard, he nearly took it off its hinges.

Janet came wide awake and jumped up to grab on to her husband. She'd never seen him this furious before.

A glance out the window told her why he was so enraged.

The black form had followed them.

All she could understand at this moment was that she had to stop Jack from confronting the black form.

Jack slammed open the door and started down the steps.

"No!" Janet cried. "You don't know what it will do to you!"

But Jack seemed not to hear her. His eyes were fixed on the

transparent black form sitting on the bench, flames from the guttering fire casting an eerie red glow over its demonic body.

In Jack's hand, Janet realized for the first time, was a bottle. A weapon.

"No!" she cried again and reached out for Jack, trying to stop him.

But it was no use. Jack shrugged off her hands and walked—stalked, really—toward the demon, which sat in plain sight as if it was waiting for Jack.

Janet: "Jack had just left the camper when it disappeared as it usually did—just vanished. I can't tell you the relief I felt. I was so proud of my husband for wanting to defend us, but at the same time I didn't want to see him hurt. I knew that his anger was just giving the demon a perfect excuse to murder him, and that's what I was praying against."

The remaining days of the camping trip went no better.

John: "Toward the end of the week Mary was very run down. Most nights we were up listening to noises on the roof or smelling the odors the thing was pushing into the camper. It took its toll, there's no doubt about that."

Dawn came to her mother one day and said: "Grandma's crying, mom. You'd better go help her."

Janet found Mary Smurl in the camper, weeping.

Janet: "You could see the effects the whole week had had on her. Her health wasn't strong to begin with, and this week had just about shattered her."

The weather wasn't helping, either. It was difficult to enjoy a week in the outdoors when a steady drizzle fell much of the time, or when the temperature slipped as low as fifty degrees.

There were two nights remaining on their planned outing. Janet asked Jack if he wanted to return to West Pittston: "Won't it be like admitting defeat, honey?"

Janet sighed, forced to agree with him.

That night Chris Moughan and Dawn heard a terrible moaning sound. Dawn: "It was like something from the grave, it really was."

Jack woke just as the moaning was subsiding. He got his flashlight and walked around the camper but found nothing.

When he returned to the camper, he found that his family had once more been wound tight to the point of breaking.

At first light, Jack went to the manager of the campground and told the man that the family was headed back home.

"Day early?" the man said.

Jack frowned. "It's been happening again."

Earlier, Jack had confided in the man what had been taking place the past few years, including the supernatural incidents that had happened here, at the campground. Jack had been afraid that the man would tell him that the Smurl family was not welcome here. Instead the man had been very sympathetic, as he was now. "Any way I can help?"

Jack smiled grimly. "I sure wish there was."

In the drizzle, the sky slate gray as in wintertime, the surrounding hills lost in a soft silver mist, the Smurl family packed up its belongings. It had not been the trip they had hoped for.

Jack fought against an anger that threatened to overwhelm him. He knew he needed to remain in control for the sake of his loved ones.

On the way back home, Carin slept with her head in Janet's lap. When she woke up, Carin began crying very softly.

Nobody had to ask why.

LORRAINE WARREN:

Ed and I had been working on another case in upstate New York when the Smurls returned home and phoned us about their experiences at the campground.

And the disturbances had only increased when they'd gotten home. The house filled with the smell of fecal matter when they first opened the door, and that was followed a few days later by an incident we had never encountered in all our years as psychic investigators.

We got Janet to describe it in detail:

Q. Do you remember anything special about that morning?

A. I was very, very tired. The trip to the campground had worn me out. This was a few days after our return and I was still in bed at ten in the morning, which was very unlike me. But for some reason, probably a combination of exhaustion and depression, I really couldn't drag myself out of bed. And that's when it happened.

Q. Can you describe it?

A. [Long pause.] I can try.

Q. It was a hand.

A. Yes. A human hand.

Q. And it came from where?

A. Right up through the mattress.

Q. A human hand right up through the mattress?

A. While I was lying there.

Q. Did it try to choke you?

A. No, it just grabbed me by the back of the neck and held me.

Q. It felt like a human hand?

A. Yes. It was very powerful, you could feel its muscles, hot and sort of—clammy, I guess, at the same time.

Q. Did you try to get away?

A. I tried but it didn't do any good.

Q. You couldn't move?

A. Right.

Q. What did you do?

A. It was very odd. I just sort of resigned myself. Always before I'd fought back but after I realized I couldn't move, I thought, what's the use. [Long pause.] Actually, I started talking to it.

Q. To the hand?

A. Yes, and to the demon that controlled the hand.

Q. What did you say?

A. I said, "I don't care what you do to me. If you want to kill me, go ahead. I'm not going to fight back or anything. I'm starting to lose my will and maybe even my sanity, so why don't you just go ahead and get it over with—take me right here and right now but leave the rest of my family alone."

Q. Then what happened?

A. The hand disappeared.

Q. Just like that?

A. Just like that.

Q. Did the haunting subside for a while then?

A. No, and that was when I realized that the demon took a great deal of pleasure in tormenting us. It enjoyed sapping our energy. In that sense it was like a vampire needing blood, only this demon needed our body heat and our spiritual energy, and it enjoyed keeping us right on the edge. All the time. Right on the edge.

215

Q. So the haunting continued?

A. Just that night the banging in the walls started again and then the next day I saw Simon sort of mysteriously drawn to our upstairs closet where the demon liked to dwell. I barely got Simon back before he went inside. And then in the bedroom later on I heard these whispers that started to become moans and I was— [long pause.]

Q. [Softly] You were what?

A. [Pause.] I was afraid I was losing my mind.

Q. The whispers, you mean?

A. Everything. You really start to doubt your own sanity. Here everything around you looks very familiar—cars and appliances and groceries—only there's something else, too, some other dimension that other people don't have to endure. And when you're exposed to that dimension long enough, well, obviously, it starts to take its toll on you and on everybody around you. Jack got home that afternoon and I was really sobbing. I just couldn't handle it anymore. He had to let me sit in his lap as if I was a little girl. I really just couldn't deal with it. There was a part of me that wished the demon had taken me up on my offer—you know, that it could take my life if it would just leave my family alone. That way there would have been peace for everybody. That way the demon would have finally left us alone. I mean, we knew after staying at the campground for a week that there was going to be no peace for us. No matter where we went, it was going to follow us [starting to cry gently] no matter where we went.

Q. It even appeared to you and your mother, didn't it?

A. Yes.

Q. Would you tell us about that?

A. [Gathers herself.] Around ten o'clock the following evening my own mother, Gloria, came to visit. We sat in the kitchen and we saw this white, almost blinding form appear on the other side of the screen door. It had the intensity of a fireworks display with a very, very white center. Gradually we saw that the longer we stared at it, the more it resembled the black form that had appeared so many times before, except this one was a white gold color. My mother held my hand the whole time the form stood there and when it vanished, she started crying. I'd rarely seen her this upset; ordinarily, she's a composed person. But then I realized how accustomed I was getting to supernatural phenomena and I had to take into account that for other people such events were overwhelming. I took my mother in my arms and held her for a very long time and then afterward we sat back down at the table and had a very intimate conversation—the intense fear that we had shared had brought us even closer, and I told her how much I loved her and cared about her and she told me the same things.

Q. At the same time, the demon was working on John Smurl, too, wasn't it?

A. Oh, yes. The next morning John was getting ready to go to work when he heard this voice say, "Don't I look sexy in bed?" Now you'd expect that the person speaking would be Mary, but of course it wasn't. Mary was asleep and John knew it. He told me he stood there for maybe two minutes almost afraid to turn around—afraid of what he would see—but when he did turn around there was nothing. Just empty space. The demon had begun imitating family voices.

Q. The demon also created a terrible new way to terrorize you, too, didn't it?

A. Yes. Striking in two places at once. While Heather was in the bathroom with Simon, it started whispering to Simon and Heather heard it, and at the exact same time, on the other side of the duplex, it appeared to Mary in the form of a very grotesque dog that scooted under her couch.

Q. It showed itself to Shannon, too?

A. [Sigh.] Shannon was asleep during a very bad electric storm and when she woke up she saw a white form, much like the one my mother and I had seen, with very "big black eyes," as she described them to us. The demon was active later that night, also, picking on Simon again. It pretended to be a cat and from inside the closet came the sounds of a cat meowing. Simon rushed to the closet door. We opened it up for him to see if in fact he had a new playmate, but it was just the demon playing tricks again. [Laugh.] Actually, if you could've seen the disappointment on Simon's face when he found out there wasn't anything in there—well, it was pretty funny.

Unfortunately, for Janet and Jack, Simon's sad face would be about the only laugh the family would enjoy for many long days afterward.

People Are Talking

*T*uesday of that week there was a phone call from the producer of the TV show "People Are Talking," inviting the Smurls to return, but Janet gently declined. Though there was increasing talk of going public, no final decision had been made. Besides, as Janet joked to Jack that night, "People are talking, anyway, whether we go on that show or not."

The Smurls were well aware of how many people in West Pittston were talking about their problems. Friends told other friends, and soon the awareness level was very high.

Sometimes, when the demon was not making her life miserable, Janet liked to sit in the front window and stare out at the children playing in the street. At these moments, she knew a peace that was rarely hers these days, the peace of being a link in a vast chain. Her mother had been a link and now she, as a mother, was a link, and someday the four girls would be links. She watched as

Carin jumped rope and sang "London Bridge." Janet wondered for how many decades or perhaps even centuries children had been singing "London Bridge," and she delighted herself for the next twenty minutes watching how the sun dappled the pavement and the grass and the shrubbery. This was August and you could see the first hints of autumn in the brown-turning hills in the distance. The air was hot but not too much so and Janet, her head on the couch, allowed herself the luxury of drifting off to sleep—until the screams from upstairs jarred her from her slumber.

She went up the stairs two at a time. Shannon had not been feeling well and had come in for a nap.

When she reached Shannon's room, out of breath and terrified, Janet saw Shannon huddled in a corner, big tears streaking her cheeks.

"A man, mommy," Shannon said.

"What man?"

"He came into the room and started taking things out of my toy box."

Janet went over and knelt next to her daughter, smoothed her hair, kissed her wet cheek. "Honey, maybe you were dreaming it."

"I wasn't asleep, mommy. I was playing. Anyway, he's come in here before."

"He has?"

Shannon nodded somberly.

"Can you describe this man for me, honey?"

"He's big and he walks sort of funny and his eyes are real dark and it—it hurts to look at him. And he smells. He smells real bad."

"Has he tried to hurt you in any way?"

"He just looks at me, mommy." She put her head on Janet's shoulder and began crying softly. "He scares me, mommy. He scares me a lot."

Going Public

By the time Jack got home that evening, Janet was on one of her "half-and-half" diets—half nicotine, half caffeine.

As he stood in the kitchen doorway observing how tightly wound his wife was, Jack sensed that she was approaching another crisis point.

She turned from the window and there were tears in her eyes.

"It was in Shannon's room again this afternoon," she said.

Jack swore.

Very quietly, she said, "It's time."

He did not have to ask what she was talking about.

"What if they laugh?"

"Then they laugh," Jack said.

"What if they call us crazy?"

"Then they call us crazy."

"What if they laugh at the children?"

The pain in his eyes was more than she could stand to look at. She dropped her gaze. "I'm sorry I said that."

"No," he said, "no, you're right. Maybe they will laugh at the kids."

"That would be hard to stand."

"But you know what would be even harder?"

"What?"

"To watch it destroy us one by one and not to fight back every way we can." He touched her hand. Evening shadows were purple in the kitchen window. The stars were bright in the hazy wash of sky. "And that means exposing it. That means forcing the diocese to get involved and that means letting everybody in the community know what's going on here, even if some people do laugh at us." He paused. "You agree?"

She did not give her answer for a very long time, and when it came, it was not even a word. It was just a nod. A simple but profound nod.

Lull Before
the Storm

*T*hey sat up long into the night, making plans. In the morning, Janet would once again try the diocese, and then she would, if the diocese office refused to help, call a staff writer for the Wilkes-Barre *Sunday Independent* named Minnie MacLellan.

In the morning, following a night without any evidence of the demon, Janet rolled over and slid her arm around her husband's side. "This is sort of like the old days," she said sentimentally.

"Peaceful," he said.

Then she nudged him and laughed. "No—hurried." She jumped out of bed and said, "Remember how we used to like to stay in bed till the very last minute and then we'd have to rush around? Well, guess what time it is?"

Jack rolled over and glanced at the clock. He had forty-five minutes to get to work. "God, I really overslept."

"You kept asking me to hit the snooze alarm."

He kissed her, laughed. "Great." Then the laugh faded. "You remember everything you're supposed to do?"

"Right."

"I sure hope the diocese just decides to go along and we don't have to go to the paper."

Stubbornly, Janet said, "I guess that'll be up to them."

He kissed her again and said. "Good luck, honey. I sure hope it works."

While Jack showered, Janet threw on a robe and went downstairs to fix his breakfast.

Janet Smurl here recounts her experience with the diocese office:

Q. You phoned the office?

A. Yes.

Q. And what were you told?

A. Basically, that they would do something to help us.

Q. Did they define what that something was?

A. They certainly gave the impression that it would be something along the lines of sending a priest out.

Q. So you didn't call the newspaper that day?

A. No.

Q. Did a priest come out?

A. No.

Q. Did you call the diocese back?

A. We talked about it but then we began to think, what's the use? All your life you're raised to believe in the kindness of the church and then you go through something like this. Well, it just drains you. That's the only way to put it. It drains you.

Q. So eventually you did go to the press?

A. Not eventually. A few days later.

Q. And you went because the church didn't offer its help?

A. That and because of what happened to Jack.

Q. And that was?

A. A succubus appeared for a second time, almost exactly one year after it had attacked the first time. It was devastating.

A Second Attack

*T*he time was dawn.

A round red summer sun was pushing up past clouds already hazy with pollutants, casting an almost bloody glow over the bedroom in which Janet and Jack Smurl slept.

And then abruptly Jack was awake.

A voluptuous young woman was on top of Jack, riding him in the position of sexual domination. Despite her beauty and the pleasure she was obviously enjoying, her eyes remained a shocking and sickly neon green.

Next to him, Janet slept. Jack knew that she was in a deep psychic sleep.

Despite his prayers, the succubus would not be contained. Still in the form of the beautiful young woman whose alabaster nakedness was only complemented by the reddish glow of the rising sun, the succubus plundered Jack sexually, sinking down and then moving up on him several times.

He exhorted the demon to be gone but he found that he was unable to move or speak.

And the succubus continued, mounting him once more, hair flying wildly, neon green eyes growing larger and more lurid as its mouth ran with the drool of satisfaction.

The curious thing was that for all the movement—and the succubus put on a dazzling show, full of tricks—Jack felt no sexual sensation at all.

He lay there and simply watched the demon perform.

And then it was over.

One moment he had been the pawn of Satan himself, and now he lay covered with a gelatinous, sticky mess, the same stuff the night hag had left on him when it had reached a climax during its first attack.

Sickened by what had happened, Jack got up from the bed and went into the shower where he stood for nearly half an hour.

He scrubbed himself until his skin ached.

Out of the shower, he covered himself with talcum powder and Aqua Velva. Then he began brushing his teeth. Obsessively. To the point that his gums began to bleed.

The Interview

*F*ollowing the reappearance of the succubus, Jack Smurl went down to the breakfast table and quietly said, "I'd like you to call that reporter Minnie MacLellan this morning."

And so it was arranged. What they'd put off for so long. What appeared to be the only thing left for the Smurls. Going public. And putting themselves at the mercy of the public and the media.

Janet: "You always hear that confession is good for the soul and that you reach a catharsis when you tell somebody something that has been troubling you a long time, but in this case—in the case of the interview, I mean—we were just kind of going through the motions.

"Minnie was very nice. She took us seriously and asked very intelligent follow-up questions and gave us plenty of time to clarify what we said."

Jack: "Ed and Lorraine backed up everything we said. They

were very helpful to us. Very helpful. I have to smile when I think back to some of Minnie's expressions. We gave her a lot of material, probably a lot more than she thought she'd get, and Ed and Lorraine gave her a very good grounding in the whole psychic experience."

Janet: "I was surprised by how sympathetic and attentive to detail she was. She really wasn't just looking for a sensational story. She wanted the truth to be told and she was willing to let us tell it our way, and so we did. We covered most of the high points of the infestation since the beginning."

Jack: "There was an inherent plea in the story for anybody who could help us to please step forward and do so. We also made a very strong appeal for the diocese to get involved again."

Janet: "I suppose we had mixed feelings when it was all over—as if we didn't know quite how to feel. On the one hand, it did feel good to just tell the facts as they'd happened and use our real name and address. That was one reason we'd decided to go with the newspaper instead of TV. We felt it would give us an opportunity to be more cautious and to make sure that what we said was what we wanted to say. When you get in front of a camera, you just can't believe the pressure that's on you."

Jack: "After the interview was finished, we sat with the Warrens and talked about what we might anticipate from the public, and we seemed to swing from optimism to pessimism. Ed kept reminding us that the public could be fickle and unpredictable but that the thing we had to keep our eye on was that we'd 'come clean' as it were and that we should feel better about that. And I guess we did, really. There had been a cleansing effect in telling our story."

Janet: "The story was due to come out on Sunday, August seventeenth. All we could do at this point was wait and see what the reaction was. As Jack said, we'd have these great highs and then great lows trying to figure out how people were going to react to us."

Jack: "We decided to go away for the weekend, to Cinnaminson, to visit Jack's sister and her husband, Betty Ann and Bill Yanovitch. The demon, to remind us that nothing had changed where it was concerned, woke me up in the middle of the night with a burning smell. I checked the Yanovitch house and found no fire or anything. Finally, I went back to bed. There were some bangings, just enough to annoy me, but eventually I got to sleep. Overall, we had a very nice weekend, mom and dad joining us for their forty-ninth wedding anniversary. The wood burning smell came one more time and I checked it out, remembering that the Warrens had said that if we smelled fire we should check it out because this smell is often created by demons and while it's usually manufactured there is the dim possibility that one time in a million it might actually *be* a fire. But it wasn't so we went back to enjoying our weekend."

Janet: "Forty-nine years of marriage is really something to celebrate and we did. It was one of the loveliest weekends we've ever had. None of us said much about the newspaper article that was going to appear. We just decided to wait till we got back home to see what happened. We'd know soon enough."

On the drive back home, the windows rolled down in the van, the rolling green countryside serene at dusk, Janet said, "Wouldn't it be nice if we found somebody waiting on our doorstep who told us exactly what to do to get rid of the demon?"

Jack laughed and patted her knee. "You don't want much, do you?"

Notoriety

*U*nderstanding, compassion, a solution to their dilemma—these were the things the Smurls had hoped that publicity would bring them.

In fact, it brought them just the opposite.

On the Sunday night when they returned from John's and Mary's anniversary celebration, they sensed an uneasiness in the neighborhood. Two of the girls remarked on this fact. "Something feels weird, mom," Dawn said as the family unloaded things from the camper and brought them inside the house. "Oh, it's just your imagination, hon," Janet said, not wanting to admit that she felt the same inexplicable anxiety.

Washing up twenty minutes later, Janet happened to glance out the window. Immediately, she called for Jack.

Her husband, always alert to trouble, appeared almost instantly.

"Everything all right?" he asked.

"Look outside."

Jack walked over to the window, and parted the frilly blue chintz curtains.

"The car," Janet said.

"The black Dodge?"

"Yes."

"What about it?"

"It's been sitting there for ten minutes."

"Wonder why?"

"There're three of them."

"Three of who?"

"Teenage boys. Two in the front seat and one in the back. And they take turns pointing to our house."

An unpleasant awareness dawned in Jack. "The article this morning."

"Right."

"My God."

"Our house," Janet said, "is going to become a tourist attraction."

Janet's prediction came true.

In the course of the next week, the Smurl family logged more than two hundred calls from journalists of every stripe—newspapers, television both local and national, radio both local and national, wire services, and supermarket tabloids.

And the three teenage boys sitting in a black Dodge pointing to the house proved to be only the start. Day and night cars filled with gawking, pointing people crawled past the duplex. Some of the faces reflected the gravity of the Smurls' situation; others smirked or scoffed.

The street itself was beginning to resemble the parking lot of a major public event, the event being housed inside the Smurl duplex.

By Friday those who merely drove by and pointed had been replaced by a more brazen breed of onlooker—these people brought beer, soda, and sandwiches and camped out on the sidewalk or on the neighbors' front lawns. Some even climbed a tree in front of the house and tried to get onto the porch to take a look inside the house from the upstairs windows.

A policeman told a local reporter: "This is like a mixture of a rock concert and a religious event. You've got people out here purely as a lark but you've also got people who are screaming and passing out and claiming that they see all sorts of sights inside the Smurl house. There are some pretty scary people here and that's why I feel sorry for the Smurls. This is the kind of crowd that can turn ugly very quickly with just the right incentive."

Twenty-four hours a day the spectators continued to move past the duplex. They came in shiny new Buicks and rusted old Plymouths, in sporty little Toyota trucks and on sleek black Harley Davidson motorcycles. Some pointed, some smirked, some blessed themselves. They were young and old, white and black, rich and poor. Some of them went around the block many times and some found a place from which they could sit or stand in the baking heat and observe the house.

West Pittston had never seen anything like this. As one town official told a network television reporter: "This is the largest private event in West Pittston's history. By Thursday of this week more than sixteen hundred cars drove past the Smurl household every day. But that was only the beginning. Cars and campers from virtually every state in the union have been parking all over West Pittston and their owners have walked over to the Smurl house. There have even been fights among the onlookers to see who got closest to the house. It's been a total zoo, so much so that on Thursday night, we ordered the police to barricade the entire street. It got that bad."

Among the thousands who had thronged to the duplex on West Pittston were teenagers who hurled beer bottles at the house and called out filthy names; a motorcycle gang with occult symbols on their jackets and menace in their eyes; and some college students who thought it was funny to walk by with big ghetto-blaster radios and play "Ghostbusters."

But this wasn't the only attention the family was attracting.

By now Janet and Jack Smurl had become instant celebrities.

Throughout the United States, major daily newspapers carried their story and their photo. From the *New York Post* to national television news shows, the Smurls had become a major story.

Of those reporters invited into the Smurl home, two reported supernatural experiences of their own while inside the house, which only heightened the impact of their stories. One complained of bitterly freezing temperatures and another of a "sickening, fetid odor." It didn't take long for reporters to understand that what was going on here was both serious and real.

By week's end even more reporters had joined the fray and were turning out "Smurl copy."

As Janet Smurl would remark later, "We've actually paid two prices—the haunting itself and the loss of our privacy. I can't tell what that first week was like; we were literally prisoners inside our own house. And some of the reporters were very insulting, questioning not just our motives but our sanity. It only increased the stress. Fortunately, we did meet a few good people, among them a woman named Judith Dirnell."

ED WARREN:

Over the years Lorraine and I had seen many supernatural events turn into media events, most notably the Brookfield, Connecticut case with its resultant murder trial, but we had seen none that had attracted such sheer frenzy.

Janet and Jack met both types of reporters, the good and the bad. The former were sympathetic, methodical, open-minded. The latter wanted the most sensational story they could get, even if it presented the Smurls in a bad light.

Just as the more cynical reporters depressed Janet and Jack, so did the crowds. There was an ugly aspect to it all—the sun beating down, a sense of madness in the eyes of the hot, sweaty gawkers—and even contempt in some of their voices, as if they were demanding that the Smurls *prove* to them that satanic forces were in fact at work here.

Lorraine and I even had words with some of the spectators. We made the mistake of simply asking a few of the pushier ones to move off the lawn and let the family have its privacy. Some of them—soaked with sweat, smelling of beer—challenged our right to make our request. It was at this moment that I saw how the demon was turning all this into yet another form of punishment for the Smurls. Looking out your window to find a stranger peering in is a very unnerving experience and one the Smurls would suffer for months.

Fortunately, among the vast media audience was a thirty-four-year-old woman named Judith Dirnell, who happened to work at the same plant where Jack did. It was she who contacted the Smurls and told them of a remarkable woman who communicated frequently with the supernatural world through a spirit she could contact at will.

The woman's name was Mary Alice Rinkman and she came over to the Smurl house on Thursday, August 21. The upshot was stunning, and provided a key clue to our ongoing investigation.

Janet: "Judith was very impressive, warm but businesslike. Shortly after she sat down on the couch, we saw her give a start. I asked her what was wrong and Judith said that something sharp but invisible had poked her in the eye, like a human thumb. Then, as she was wiping the tears from her eyes, her head jerked up and she pointed to something by the staircase. We asked her what it was and she then proceeded to describe perfectly the black form that had haunted us for nearly two years.

"Her eye continued to swell. Finally she had to go home and put an ice pack on it. She returned later that night with Mary Alice Rinkman, who had a very serious aura about her. We could see that she was very aware of what was going on here and was also very concerned. She asked to be taken through all the rooms in the house and then down into the basement, which was where she came into contact with a spirit named Abigail.

"Mary Alice was in a state of trance, her eyes closed and her fingers trembling. She said: 'Abigail is elderly and she's either senile or confused but she isn't harmful.' Then Mary Alice went on to describe Abigail in exactly the same terms Lorraine had months earlier.

"Twenty minutes later, when Mary Alice asked to be taken to the middle bedroom upstairs, we saw how exactly her sense of the haunting matched Lorraine's, because Mary Alice then started to describe another spirit she was seeing, a man with a mustache named Patrick, who she said had died here but was afraid to return to the other side.

"Mary Alice, lost in another trance, then began to give us some background on Patrick. He was a man who often beat his wife Elizabeth somewhere near the Smurl property before the house was built. This was sometime in the nineteenth century.

"Whenever Elizabeth became afraid of Patrick, she became involved with another man. One day Patrick came home unexpectedly and found Elizabeth in the embrace of her lover. He killed both of them, strangling Elizabeth and beating the man to death with his fists. Mary Alice then described how Patrick was beaten by a mob and then hung for the murders. And then she turned to me and said something we'd never expected.

" 'Janet, you look like Elizabeth. Patrick thinks Jack is your lover and he wants you and Jack separated.'

"As she told us this, a vase began to rattle, and then sharp rappings were heard in the wall.

"Mary Alice, in a strange, deep voice, began to implore Patrick to 'go to the other side,' but she told us that he was afraid he'd be punished if he crossed into the other realm.

"When Mary Alice came out of her trance, she said, very matter of factly, 'Patrick doesn't want to leave this house. It will be very difficult to get rid of him.'

"Then Mary Alice paused, looking very distressed and said, 'But that isn't the worst news. There's more, I'm afraid.' She shook her head, almost as if she were afraid to give voice to what she was thinking. 'There's a third earthbound spirit here—it could be either a man or a woman, I'm not sure—but whatever it is, it's violent and vicious and means to harm you.' She then explained that this spirit was insane and if it were alive today would be institutionalized in a mental hospital. 'This is the malevolent spirit that controls Patrick and continues to urge him to do violence. This is the spirit that wants the demon to commit the ultimate atrocity—possession of one or both of you.' Her eyes stared at midpoint in the room and her voice became even huskier. 'Then there is the demon itself, a direct disciple of the Devil's. I sense it throughout the house. Everywhere.'"

The look that passed between Janet and Jack was heartbreaking because once again the most disturbing possibility had been mentioned—the spectre of possession, of a demon literally taking control of a living person. Would it be one of them? One of their children?

No Mercy

*I*n the following two weeks the Smurl family saw the human species at its best and worst.

Many people stopped by the house and offered them rosaries and other religious items. From all over the world came cards and letters wishing them well and including special prayers and suggestions about how to handle their haunting. Clergymen of every denomination contacted them and offered them prayers—all except (for the present anyway) a representative of the diocese.

Jack: "One thing that was reassuring about the mail was that we heard from so many people who had had experiences similar to ours. And I mean people from everywhere—Brazil, Puerto Rico, the Netherlands, and many other European countries. That made us feel a little less isolated."

Janet: "There was no rest for us. During this time when the press surrounded our house, the haunting continued, usually in the form of rappings or the fleeting appearance of the dark form, while down on our kitchen table the telegrams and messages stacked up. We put them in grocery bags and in boxes and piled them in the kitchen closet; we just kept running out of room. Fortunately, since most of the messages contained information and good wishes and religious medals, they were encouraging rather than discouraging."

But certainly there *were* things to be discouraged about.

Even on Friday, August 22, when West Pittston recorded a significant amount of rainfall, the crowds were merciless, pushing closer, closer, trying for a look inside or to touch family members as they tried to leave the house.

Jack: "Some people were convinced we were holy and other people were convinced we were messengers from Satan. The latter got very bad when we heard from a coven of witches who wanted to come over and meet us. That's just what we needed at that time—witches!"

The people on the street began to display even more bizarre behavior.

Janet: "Two incidents really disturbed us. One morning a man holding a handgun drove past our house very slowly. We happened to be looking out the window at the time and we ducked down, afraid of what he might do. Another man got very close to our front door with a huge machete in his hand. Luckily, several people in the crowd shouted at him and he ran off.

"But of all the things that happened during the time of the crowds, probably the most depressing was the phone call from a woman I'd considered a friendly acquaintance if not an outright friend of mine. Our daughters were in school together—school would start in a few weeks—but she called me one evening and said that she didn't want her daughter to be friends with mine any more. That really hurt."

The reporters had become so overwhelming in their numbers and demands that on August 23, at 2:00 P.M. exactly, Janet and Jack stood on their back porch and read a prepared statement to the throng.

"As reporters, you can see that this situation has gotten completely out of hand. No one is helping us with our problems, we can't keep up with all the calls and letters, and we don't know how to handle this situation. Please say a prayer for us in church."

Temporarily at least, the reporters pulled back from the house and gave the Smurls some privacy. But that privacy was not to last long.

The Haunting Widens

*T*he call came at dusk. The caller was a neighbor. She was not angry but she was afraid, very afraid.

"Janet, it's affecting all of us," she said.

"I know it," Janet said, fearing what her friend was going to say next.

"Six separate houses, including mine."

"Supernatural things, you mean?"

"Rappings. Bad odors. Screams."

"I'm sorry," Janet said, feeling the last of her energy and hope draining from her.

Now the demon was using their friends and neighbors to make the haunting even more terrible.

The woman said, "I didn't call to make you feel bad, Janet. I just wondered if there was any advice you could give us."

Janet smiled bitterly to herself. "If I had any to give, I would have taken it myself a long time ago."

The woman laughed sadly. "I guess that's right, isn't it?"

"I'll pray for you," Janet said.

That night, watching TV, the Smurls saw something that surprised them. The anchorman on WNEP announced that the station had taken a poll to see how many viewers believed the Smurls' story and how many viewers disbelieved it.

The results were amazing: 75 percent believed the Smurls and only 25 percent doubted them.

Janet: "I suppose it was silly to feel good about that but after everything that had happened to us, it was nice to know that the majority of people in the community saw us as sane and honest. It was comforting to know that."

In the middle of the night, Jack Smurl got up to go to the bathroom. Before going back to bed, he glanced at himself in the mirror. What he saw caused him to jerk backward as if he'd been shot.

The face in the mirror belonged not to him but to a decomposed man whose flesh hung in tatters and whose eyes burned with the sorrow of the newly dead.

Then the image was gone and his own face was back.

For the remainder of the night, Jack lay in bed thinking of one word again and again: *possession.*

Is that what he would look like if the demon succeeded in completing the fourth stage of the haunting—possession?

He thought of what Mary Alice had described to him. He thought of what Ed and Lorraine Warren had said was the demon's ultimate goal.

Then he thought of the ghoul he'd seen in the mirror—the feral, glistening eyes, the rotting flesh, the twisted, skeletal hand.

Had it been a premonition of what he himself was about to become? Daylight was a long time coming.

LORRAINE WARREN:

At long last Ed and I were glad to see that at least one goal of the Smurls' going public had paid off—they heard from the diocese office, though unfortunately not in the way they'd hoped.

Janet told us, "Father Mullally from the diocese bureau was not pleased that we'd given our story to the press. He said that we should have contacted the church first—as if we hadn't. We simply told him that, given all the things that were going on, we couldn't wait any longer, that our lives were now hanging in the balance.

"The diocese office was not pleased that they were getting so many calls from reporters asking about our case.

"Finally, a few days after the call from Father Mullally, a priest came out and talked to us. We told him about the previous exorcisms and how the diocese had refused to help. We also expressed our resentment that a newspaper story the day before had given the impression that we'd never tried to contact the Scranton diocese office until recently. He was very polite but he was careful to express neither belief nor disbelief in what we told him. At the end of the interview he was very cordial and said he'd get back to us.

"We did not hear from the Scranton diocese for several days, though meanwhile a priest from another diocese offered to perform an exorcism. Then he called back and said that the Scranton office, which had heard of his offer, called him and said that for him to come into the Scranton diocese would break protocol. Wonderful!"

By this time Ed and I had begun to chart the subtle but certain shift in ferocity the supernatural attacks displayed. We also noted Jack's somewhat different demeanor—pale skin, anxious glances—and what appeared to be his clinical depression. This worried us greatly. We discussed this with Linda Fedele, a team member of ours who is also a detective with the Norwalk, Connecticut, police department, and she went and visited the Smurls. She confirmed our fears about Jack's condition. Though we didn't use the word with Linda, what we were concerned about was that the demon, which might well be jealous of Jack, seeing him as a rival for Janet's love, might in fact be in the process of trying to possess him.

There was no doubt that drastic action had to be taken, and quickly.

We spent two long days brainstorming with team members. The result was a plan for a mass exorcism that would involve several priests. To tell the Smurls of our plan, Doctor Anthony Giangrasso, a former medical examiner now in private practice, and his wife Bettie, of Trumble, Connecticut went to the Smurl duplex.

Doctor Giangrasso, who has been our friend for more than twenty years and who has worked with us on many cases, reported back to us that he was quite moved by his interview with Janet and Jack and that what made the situation so startling for him was that the haunting was not limited (as it usually was) to just a few people but extended to dozens of people who were, in various respects, linked to the Smurls.

While we were talking to the doctor and his wife, the phone rang. Ed answered it in the other room. When he came back, he looked upset. He said, "I'm told the Scranton diocese isn't going to help us with our mass exorcism."

He didn't have to say any more than that.

At the moment, that was about the worst news the Smurls could have received.

The Diocese Declines

*T*rue to the priest's promise, the Scranton diocese finally did call the Smurls back. Indeed, the office requested that Janet and Jack meet with Father Mullally in his own office the following afternoon.

The Smurls were very hopeful that Father Mullally had good news for them, bouyed as they were by the fact that as autumn began to touch the trees and thin the summer sunlight, the crowds camped outside had thinned somewhat.

Not that the press itself had lost interest in the Smurl story. Janet: "We were still on the news several times a week and we lost count of how many hundreds of new stories had been filed about us. But happily some of the freakish nature of the investigation had quieted down. With the call from the diocese, we had new hope that some serious steps were finally going to be taken and that perhaps our problem would be resolved once and for all."

Twenty-four hours later Janet and Jack sat in Father Mullally's office explaining the mass exorcism plan the Warrens had suggested. The Smurls were anxious for the diocese to talk to the Warrens.

The chancellor, also present at the meeting, stunned the couple when he said that there was no reason whatsoever to talk to the Warrens because from this point on the diocese itself was taking over the investigation.

"But Ed and Lorraine have been a tremendous help to us," Janet said. "We haven't met anybody who understand the supernatural better than the Warrens."

But the chancellor shook his head. The diocese would be taking over the investigation. As far as the official church was concerned, the Warrens were no longer involved.

ED WARREN:

Lorraine and I were not surprised at the response of the church. Like all institutions, Catholicism has its own priorities and obviously, in this case, the chancellor felt that the most important thing to do was quiet the negative publicity over how the diocese office had treated the Smurls in the past.

Our one reservation was that we knew how the church worked in such cases, the object being to find a "scientific explanation" for hauntings whenever possible, sometimes to the exclusion of the real explanation.

As for the Smurls, nothing got any easier for them."

INTERVIEW WITH MAUREEN COWLES

Q. You've been a good friend of the Smurls?

A. Very good. They're wonderful people.

Q. Would you tell us how you became involved in the haunting?

A. [Pause.] I—it was because I telephoned Janet over a weekend.

Q. Could you explain?

A. Well, they'd gone camping, which I hadn't known about, so I just kept calling to see if she wanted to get together and do some shopping.

Q. Would you elaborate on what happened then?

A. [Pause.] This little girl answered.

Q. Little girl?

A. Yes. She sounded as if she was probably seven or eight. And then she'd laugh.

Q. Laugh?

A. That was the eeriest part. Her laugh. She'd say, "They don't live here any more." And then she'd hang up. I called six or seven times that weekend. I just couldn't believe what I was hearing. But the little girl would always answer. I even called the operator to verify the number but she said that it was the Smurl house I was calling.

Q. And you told Janet?

A. Sure. Right away. She got as scared as I was. With everything her family was going through, they didn't need some new kind of trouble like this.

Jack: "Despite the efforts of the church to carry on its own plans, Janet and I felt that it was important for us to carry on with ours—namely a prayer meeting organized by our friends and by fifty women and twenty men of the Sacred Heart League of St. Mary's Annunciation in Kingston, which is near West Pittston."

By the time these people, and other family friends, filled the Smurl home, the mood was solemn. The days of the circuslike atmosphere of press and publicity had faded and now the Smurls were in a new era—trying to stop the demon from taking possession.

The house was transformed. Vigil candles were set out every few feet and then lit, bathing the entire house in a shadowy glow as the voices of faithful rose in communal prayer like the one the early Christians said in the catacombs. In some eyes you could see tears; on some lips, smiles, because you had the sense that the Devil was being driven out. (At a gathering later on, two people even reported seeing an image of the Blessed Virgin somehow being projected onto one of the walls, a faint but perfect impression of the Holy Mother bringing her own special powers to help drive out the demon.)

Janet: "It was a very moving spectacle—all these concerned, caring people doing everything they could to help us. You could feel the love, you really could. I had tears in my eyes most of the time. And the house looked so beautiful with the vigil lights splashing different colors across everything."

The faithful stayed till very late. But after several hours of calm and quiet, the television in the Smurls' bedroom began to rock from side to side and pounding in the walls became so violent that Janet had to cover her ears. Sobbing, she said, "Are they ever going to leave us alone? Ever?"

ED WARREN:

Janet and Jack continued to call us frequently as we waited to see what the church would do. They also continued to hear from religious people from all over the world, some responsible and tender people, others strident and threatening.

Finally, they even heard from the Scranton diocese, which agreed to dispatch a priest in the person of Monsignor Eugene Clark. It would be the monsignor's task to stay at the Smurl residence overnight and see if he could find any hard evidence of a true haunting.

Though we said nothing at the time to Janet and Jack as they excitedly told us about this, we knew that the demon would probably choose not to expose itself, thereby making the Smurls appear to the priest as either frauds or hysterics.

And that's what happened.

Diocesan priests came to the Smurl house a few times, some to stay overnight while the family slept, but none heard or saw anything that endorsed the notion that a bona fide haunting was going on here.

Jack: "That was the irony. We'd struggled so long to get the church involved, but we'd never thought about it turning out this way. Here we'd made all these claims and the church couldn't find any proof to back them up."

Things were going so badly that Jack had lost twenty pounds since the family had gone public. Janet had not only lost weight—fourteen pounds—she had also developed an ulcer.

One day, as we were talking to Janet and Jack in their living room, I began to sense the presence of the demon itself. Once again, in a way I cannot articulate, I sensed that it had grown bolder and stronger and was ready to strike.

Lorraine saw how upset I was and as soon as we'd reached the van, she said, "You look terrible."

"As soon as we get back I'm going to call Father McKenna."

We rushed back to our home and got the priest on the phone.

Ugly Incident

*A*s if to remind the Smurls that
their enemies were not just of the supernatural variety, one night
they were sitting home watching TV when Jack heard a car slow
down in front of the duplex.

By now, of course, he'd gotten used to people cruising by in
slow-moving cars. Even though public attention had dwindled,
there was still a steady flow of the curious.

"What is it, honey?" Janet asked.

"Somebody parked out there."

"Circus time again," Janet said.

But her gentle sarcasm ended abruptly when a beer bottle
came hurtling through their front window.

Jack: "All the girls were crying and huddled in the corner. It
was like there were two sieges going on—the demon, and a few
sick people who hated us for some inexplicable reason. I got a look
at the people. They were teenagers. And I called the police. But

the incident really left its mark on the family—scared us and made us very angry all over again—and so we had to rely more than ever on Ed's and Lorraine's plan to try to end the infestation. I can't say we had much hope at that point, but hope was about all we had."

The Final Exorcism

Not even Father McKenna could summon many smiles on the day, a week later, when he drove back to the Smurl residence and performed the third exorcism.

Earlier in the morning, just before driving over, Father McKenna had said a special mass for the Smurls and so, that done, the exorcism consisted of saying special prayers on both sides of the duplex and then going through each room with holy water. This time, the priest even blessed the back yard.

Janet: "Father McKenna's face was so beautiful. You could see the concentration on it. He was in effect putting his own soul on the line for this to work."

There were no disruptions during this exorcism. So impassioned were Father McKenna's prayers that the demon seemed almost afraid to show itself.

Finished, the priest once more started to his car, refusing the dinner the Smurls offered. Fasting was an integral part of the exorcism ritual, the priest reminded them.

What followed was an almost daily pilgrimage to the Smurl residence, this time by friends and relatives of the Smurl family, including the men of the Sacred Heart League. Prayers and vigil candles were strong on the air. It was Ed's and Lorraine's idea to "drown" the demon in prayer following the exorcism.

And it began to work.

Jack: "You could feel something, the way air changes after a storm has passed. At first we were almost afraid to hope that the prayers and the vigil would help in any lasting way, but overall the days following the exorcism were great. We hadn't been that relaxed in over two years."

The nice thing was, for the time being, there would be no surprises—at least not bad ones. Indeed, the one surprise the Smurls received in late September was a very pleasant one.

ED WARREN:

Janet called us a few minutes after she woke up. "You won't believe it!" she said to Lorraine and me. "The whole house is filled with the scent of roses again."

Even I had to take that as a good sign, and I say "even I" because experience has shown that it is sensible to be skeptical where hauntings are concerned. Under most circumstances, it takes a great deal of effort (either planned or inadvertent) to stir the demon and then it is nearly impossible to get rid of it.

Still, I had to admit that the extraordinary holiness shown by Father McKenna, and the daily prayers taking place at the Smurl house, were apparently quelling the forces of darkness.

And things only got better.

Janet: "We just couldn't believe it. Two, then three, then four weeks went by without a single incident. Every few days the smell of roses would return to one or two of the rooms and our house would be filled with the sound of prayer. It was wonderful and you could see the wonder on the faces of our children. They started having friends over again and planning parties and you could hear their laughter all over the house."

The press, of course, was still interested in what was going on at the Smurl house and asked for a report. In a joint statement on October twenty-eighth, Janet and Jack Smurl announced: "For several weeks now all has been quiet in our house and it would appear that our problem has been resolved."

A spokesperson for the diocese said that after an intensive investigation, the diocese had reached no conclusions and had taken no position on the case but that, since the Smurls said the matter had been resolved, the diocesse was closing its inquiry.

Gray November came but for the Smurls it had the feel of the most beautiful of springs, because in the walls there were no rappings. On the air there was no grim slaughterhouse odor. On the faces of their children were the normal smiles of youth.

Jack: "We didn't quit praying, of course. If anything, we became even more religious. We didn't want our newfound freedom to be destroyed again."

The Return

After Thanksgiving, the Smurl family began planning for Christmas. They had already been given the best gift of all, their peace of mind, but now they wanted to plan a holiday that would let them thank God and also celebrate their unity as a family.

It was a good time for them. Janet and Jack began regaining some of their lost weight, and they both eased into spending even more time with the girls and school activities.

No, you couldn't ask for a better time than this.

Jack enjoyed resting in his favorite chair. Sometimes, watching TV, he'd doze off, especially following a hard day's work.

Tonight he'd done exactly that, slept for perhaps half an hour. Now he was awake again. Johnny Carson was on, the monologue particularly funny tonight. Jack decided watching Carson would be a good way to get completely relaxed before going upstairs to bed.

With the holidays less than two weeks away, the living room was aglow with lights from the Christmas tree, beautiful, soft greens and yellows and reds. The air was scented with the clean tang of the fir tree itself.

Then he clicked off the TV and began to pray. As he did so, he glanced up at the mirror over the sofa, and he saw it—the black, caped form whose presence had announced the haunting to begin with. Only this time there was a difference.

Jack sensed the demon beckoning to him—summoning him, really—and he knew instantly what this signified: the final, dreaded stage of a haunting—possession.

He bolted from the chair, keeping his rosary tight in his hand.

The black figure started toward him.

Jack scrambled to the stairs and started backing up them slowly so he could keep the demon in his sight.

The black figure grew ever closer.

Jack's heart hammered; he was drenched in sweat. Twice he stumbled and desperately clutched at the banister for support.

The caped figure continued to move closer, closer.

Then Jack, sensing that the demon would lunge at him, took his rosary and showed it to the creature. He also began to say over and over the prayer the Warrens had taught him.

Only gradually did the demon withdraw.

Jack's voice got louder and louder, his prayer more and more intense. Then, before his eyes, the dark creature faded into the wall and disappeared.

Jack determined not to mention this to his wife or the children. He wanted them to think that things were still fine, that the scent of roses would stay, and that life would be simple and good and normal.

But in the middle of the night, bangings broke out in the walls, and on John and Mary's side of the duplex the flooring trembled violently, as if an earthquake were taking place.

The haunting had begun all over again.

* * *

There could be no mistake about it. The demon and spirits had only been waiting for the opportunity to strike again and continue their unrelenting assault on the family.

With their return, the entities used some new tactics. The flooring on John and Mary's side trembled violently, and when Mary was in the bathroom a distorted white mass about three feet tall and covered with oozing pustules rushed past her and disappeared into the vanity.

Over the next weeks, there was sharp decline in the health of the senior Smurls and the Smurl children had slipped back into anxiety and depression. Every night now, the family was haunted.

By New Year's Day, 1987, an atmosphere of terror once more filled the Smurl house.

On January 10, the girls went to bed early and Janet and Jack soon followed. They had been asleep less than half an hour when the pounding began. If you listened carefully, you could hear not only the invisible fists of old, but strange new whispers and traces of laughter.

Demonic laughter.

Janet and Jack lay awake all night, holding hands and weeping.

ED AND LORRAINE WARREN:

Today, the haunting continues.

We wish we knew why. Even more, we wish we had a solution.

Would a permanent move help the Smurls? Perhaps. Will the haunting continue all their lives? Possibly. Will the family be able to withstand the stress? We hope so.

As demonologists, neither of us can ever recall a haunting of such tenacity. The demon simply will not be displaced. It has focused its very essence on the Smurl family and will not let go.

We are still in contact with the Smurls, usually once a week. So is Father (now Bishop) McKenna. Occasionally one of our research team has an idea, which we try, but to date nothing has been successful.

There is still, of course, the terrible prospect of possession, for that is the ultimate goal of all hauntings. Jack in particular is well aware of this for it is Jack whom the demon seems most to despise.

As for any closing words of optimism, we can only reflect on what Bishop McKenna has said—that the experience of the Smurls should erase any doubts nonbelievers might have that the spirit world exists. All you have to do is stand in the Smurl home to know that demons are a very real and very dangerous part of reality.

The biggest gift we can offer the Smurls is our continued faith and our prayers that some day their burden will be lifted and the scent of roses will fill their home permanently.

Today

*T*he Smurls live as quietly as possible, liked and admired for what they have endured, fearful that the haunting that has plagued them will never end.

To be sure, there is laughter in the Smurl household. There is also pride and hope and real joy.

But always in the corners of the night there is the prospect that the demon will come and perhaps one day dominate their lives even more terribly.

There is no doubt that their story is true. Too many witnesses, and too much corroboration, have supported their ominous tale.

All that feeds their hope these days is that God in his kindness will end their ordeal. Soon.

Postscript

Just as this book went to press, the Smurl family moved from the Chase Street duplex. They now live in a quiet nearby Pennsylvania suburban community.

133.09   29038

Curran
(The) Haunted